Praise for
Good and Angry

"*Good and Angry* is a great book on how to use our anger, resolve our anger, and heal our bitter roots and resentments."
— STEPHEN ARTERBURN, author of numerous books including
Every Man's Battle (with Fred Stoeker)

"*Good and Angry* delivers a powerful combination of can-do parenting strategies and real-life scenarios from the front lines. With uncommon ease and readability, Turansky and Miller communicate solid principles that are both believable and sound."
— JULIE ANN BARNHILL, author of numerous books including
She's Gonna Blow! Real Help for Moms Dealing with Anger

"I've been selling Christian books for almost thirty years, and I have never seen a parenting book as practical, realistic, and easy to use as this one. Most busy parents don't need more theory, but they need useful tools. Implementing the techniques in this book will help children respond to life in the future."
— LANDO KLASSEN, CBA Canada board member,
Christian retailer, and father

"In *Good and Angry*, Scott Turansky and Joanne Miller demonstrate over and over that at the core of positive and rewarding parenting is working out relational routines in everyday life to prepare children's hearts to respond to the Father ⋯ ⋯iritual and life training at its most practical—traction for e⋯ ⋯ to bring up kids who follow after God."
— LORILEE CRAKER, au⋯ ⋯ Names
and *When the Belly Button ⋯*

"*Good and Angry* provides practical help to parents of kids of all ages. Turansky and Miller give parents a biblical game plan that is unusually insightful. This balanced approach to parenting will help any parent avoid the pitfalls we all fear falling into."

—Dennis Rainey, executive director of FamilyLife

Dear Reader,

Try the strategies and routines in this book. If you don't see a reduction in your anger, then return the book along with your sales receipt to:

Effective Parenting
76 Hopatcong Dr.
Lawrenceville, NJ 08648

We will give you a full refund.

If, on the other hand, the strategies work for you, why not visit our Web site (www.effectiveparenting.org) and check out some of the other resources we have for parents. We are committed to your parenting success.

Blessings,

GOOD and ANGRY

EXCHANGING FRUSTRATION FOR CHARACTER. . . IN YOU AND YOUR KIDS

SCOTT TURANSKY, D.MIN. & JOANNE MILLER, R.N., B.S.N.

SHAW BOOKS
an imprint of WATERBROOK PRESS

Good and Angry
A SHAW BOOK
PUBLISHED BY WATERBROOK PRESS
2375 Telstar Drive, Suite 160
Colorado Springs, Colorado 80920
A division of Random House, Inc.

All Scripture quotations, unless otherwise indicated, are taken from the *Holy Bible,
New International Version®*. NIV®. Copyright © 1973, 1978, 1984 by International
Bible Society. Used by permission of Zondervan Publishing House. All rights reserved.
Scripture quotations marked (KJV) are taken from the *King James Version.*

The names of persons who have come to Effective Parenting for counseling have
been changed. Some illustrations and letters are a combination of individual stories
to protect confidentiality.

Stories of the authors' children are used by permission.

ISBN 0-87788-030-1

SHAW BOOKS and its aspen leaf logo are trademarks of WaterBrook Press, a division
of Random House, Inc.

Library of Congress Cataloging-in-Publication Data

Turansky, Scott, 1957–
    Good and angry : exchanging frustration for character— in you and
your kids! / Scott Turansky, Joanne Miller.— 1st ed.
        p. cm.
    ISBN 0-87788-030-1
    1. Child rearing—Religious aspects—Christianity. 2. Anger—Religious aspects—
Christianity. 3. Parents—Religious life. I. Miller, Joanne, 1960– II. Title.
    BV4529 .T87 2002
    248.8'45—dc21

                                                        2002006632

Printed in the United States of America
2004

10 9 8 7 6 5 4

Contents

Hello,

I'm Scott Turansky. My wife, Carrie, and I have five children: Josh, Melissa, Ben, Elizabeth, and Megan. We have certainly influenced our children over the years, but they have taught us a lot as well. God has used our kids to help us grow and to reveal weaknesses in us that need attention. We've learned things like how much patience we have or don't have and better ways to handle conflict. Just the other day, I was helping our daughter Megan with math. She wasn't catching the idea, and I was getting frustrated. She gently said, "Dad, you're getting loud." She was right. I took a deep breath and tried again with a more gentle voice. Family life has taught me humility in more ways than I want to admit, but I wouldn't trade it for anything. I love my wife and my children, and we are all in this together, learning to be the people God wants us to be.

Scott Turansky

Hi,

I'm Joanne Miller, and my husband is Ed. We have two sons, Dave and Tim, who are full of energy, thoughtfulness, and fun. Our family enjoys working and playing together as we homeschool and serve in our church. I am also a pediatric nurse. My love for children and desire to see families relate together successfully goes back as far as I can remember.

The Millers and Turanskys have been friends and partners in ministry since our children were very young. Scott, Carrie, Ed, and I have enjoyed watching our kids grow up together. One day, my son Dave was talking to Scott's son Josh about the parenting seminars that we teach. Josh teasingly said, "You know, Dave, you're not the only one that learns from your mistakes. Hundreds of other families learn from your mistakes." Life is funny sometimes. We are grateful for the opportunities God has given us to serve him.

Joanne Miller

Man's anger does not bring about
the righteous life that God desires.

JAMES 1:20

"How Did We Get into This Mess Anyway?"

Avoiding the Boxing Ring

Dear Scott and Joanne,

I swore I would never become a "yeller," but I did. I was shocked with myself. I heard other parents yell at their kids and just couldn't believe they could do that. But when it was my turn, I never gave it a second thought. My daughter is extremely strong-willed, and I always thought I'd have a "good little girl." She threw me for a loop and I wasn't prepared. I just didn't know what to do. Any hint of whining, arguing, bickering, or just plain defiance would send me into one of my tirades. I knew I was just letting off steam and that I was damaging my relationship with her, but I didn't know what else to do, and I was so upset I didn't even care.

Now that my daughter is seven and my son is five, I've finally figured out that yelling isn't the answer. When my daughter yells at her brother, it sounds just like me. I cringe when I hear it. Because of your materials and the Lord's help, I'm making some significant changes, and I can't believe the difference. I'm learning some new ways of relating to my children and strategies for helping them to be more godly. Most importantly, I'm seeing how God's power is so practical in family life and that I, as a mom, can lead my children to follow the Lord.

—Laura from Billings, Montana

When children are unhappy they look for ways to draw their parents into a fight. Kids know just where your buttons are and how to push them to make you angry. "Dad wouldn't do it that way" or "You never let me have fun" might be all that's needed to create the volcano effect. When children get angry and are looking for a fight, it's as if they step into the boxing ring and invite you to join them.

All too often parents, believing that they are stronger, smarter, and more powerful, are willing to put on the gloves and enter the ring to "teach this kid a lesson" or "put him in his place." The key indicator that says you want to accept the invitation to fight is your harshness. When you respond to a situation with anger, you get into the ring and become an opponent to your child. The intensity increases as each party is determined to win the battle. Sarcasm, mean words, bringing up the past, "you always" or "you never," and an ever-increasing volume become the blows used to weaken the opponent. When it's over, parents often think they've won because they have more techniques and tricks than the child ever realized.

Unfortunately, setting ourselves up as opponents does more damage to the relationship than we expect. When our anger becomes a form of revenge, it gets in the way of God's work. Entering the boxing ring hinders the Holy Spirit's movement in our relationship with our children and prevents true change from taking place in a child's heart.

Here's what's going on behind the scenes: When a child begins mistreating a parent with arguing, meanness, or defiance, that child will feel many emotions, but especially guilt. People don't like to feel guilty, and one of the easiest ways to excuse the guilt is to justify it by looking at the sins of others. When you join the boxing match, your children feel attacked and find it easier to blame you rather than focus on what they did wrong. Blame overshadows their awareness of guilt. Romans 12:19 says, "Do not take revenge, my friends, but leave room for God's wrath." God's wrath in a person's life often comes in the form of guilt and conviction. As parents, we need to stay out of the boxing ring and allow the Holy Spirit to convict our children of sin.

Instead of getting into the ring with your children, imagine going around the ring to the child's corner and becoming a coach. You might say, "I'm not going to discuss this with you while you're upset. First, you need to settle down, and then we'll talk about the problem." Or, "The way you're talking to me sounds like you're trying to provoke me into an argument. I'm not going to fight with you." These kinds of statements set the issue aside for the moment and bring the relational dynamics to the forefront. One dad, Mike, found this boxing ring illustration particularly helpful in his relationship with his teenage son, Kyle. "It seemed as if Kyle and I fought about everything. Whenever he would challenge the things I said, I felt compelled to prove I was right. I'd have to show him the holes in his logic. Battles got pretty fierce and usually ended up with both of us feeling attacked.

"Now when Kyle challenges me, I picture the boxing ring and determine not to get inside. I continue to discipline, set limits, and dialogue, but I refuse to follow the old routine of arguing. Sometimes

I have to just keep quiet and pray that God will reveal truth to Kyle. As I've changed my response, I can see Kyle's changing too. I think he's beginning to see that I'm not going to fight and he's not trying to provoke me in the same ways."

Coaching children out of the boxing ring means that we stop dealing with the issue at hand and instead discuss the way we're relating. Moving our focus from the issue to the process has a dramatic effect on the relationship when things begin to get tense. The parent refuses to become a sparring partner and instead looks for ways to improve the relationship. This doesn't mean that the child will instantly become responsive, but it does mean that the parent chooses a different posture, one that offers healing instead of antagonism, and closeness instead of distance.

THE POWER OF ROUTINE

Getting into the boxing ring can become a pattern—a routine that you and your child easily fall into. Although it's amazing that children of all ages can figure out how to get their parents angry, it's even more startling to see how fast many parents join the fight. Sometimes you look at a teen and a parent arguing at the shopping mall and you say to yourself, "Who's the kid here?" A routine has begun. They're into it before they even realize what happened.

We all have routines in our lives that we may or may not be aware of. People are creatures of habit. We develop patterns of behavior to make our lives predictable. We may follow a similar schedule each morning, choose the same route to work, and conform to habits in the way we wash our clothes, shop for food, or even brush our teeth. Even those who consider themselves spontaneous and resistant to ruts choose routines that make life easier so they can concentrate on more important things.

We also set routines for our children because we know that they do best with consistency. A regular bedtime, for example, can help a child who struggles with moodiness. Knowing what to expect in the morning can help children keep on track and get everything done. You teach your five-year-old how to interrupt you graciously when you're talking with the neighbor and your ten-year-old what to do when his older brother starts teasing. These are all routines that dictate how one responds to the various challenges of life.

Consider these scenarios: A busy father comes home from work hoping to relax with his wife and enjoy his children. Instead, he walks into a land mine of relational issues. Children are bickering and Mom is frazzled. Even the dog has retreated to a quieter room in the house. Likewise, a mom comes home from work wanting to share a couple of interesting stories with her family only to find that, instead, everyone wants a piece of her.

When you hit those challenging moments in parenting, how do you respond? You probably have certain routines you use in conflict situations or when you're stressed or upset. One mom tells us, "I call it my 'take charge mode.' I just start taking control of everything, giving orders, solving problems, and managing people. Unfortunately, I don't do it in a gracious way. I become more interested in reestablishing my authority than in building relationships." A dad admitted, "When things get tense in my home, I retreat. I know that's not the best, but it's the way I've always responded to conflict."

You already have many subtle routines in your family. Whether it's how a child reacts when asked to follow a simple instruction or how you engage in fun after dinner, patterns of behavior teach family members what to expect. As a parent, you have a strong influence on how a dialogue takes place or when a heated conversation takes a break. These patterns develop into predictable routines of family life. Often these routines are in the background, and we don't even realize they're there until we have a problem. I (Joanne) remember when Dave was just a toddler. He wasn't a very good eater and had a hard time sitting still in his highchair. We discovered that he did pretty well, however, when he was distracted by the television. Over time, we began to allow Dave to watch Sesame Street on TV while we fed him. It became a routine that helped mealtime go more smoothly, but it had other complications we didn't yet realize. The problem came when we took a trip to Ed's parents' house and there was no Ernie and Bert to watch during breakfast. What seemed like a helpful routine had turned into an unhelpful dependency.

When routines go wrong, as they do at some point in all families, they need to be replaced with healthier ways of relating. To make lasting positive changes in our routines, we first must recognize how they can become distorted.

A GOD OF ORDER

Many of the patterns in family life reveal selfishness on the part of both the parents and the children. Angry exchanges, bad attitudes, sarcastic remarks, harsh orders, and bickering are routines that may have crept in over time and bring discouragement to everyone.

Look at a few habits that frustrate parents. Every time Dad says, "It's time to go," his two boys race to the car for the best seat. Whenever Jessica, age twelve, is asked to help with chores she groans and complains. Peter always argues when he doesn't get the answer he wants from his mom. No one can remember when these patterns started, but now they've become the routines that challenge parents on a day-to-day basis—and often lead both parent and child into the boxing ring.

As Christians, we believe that the struggles families face are part of an age-old problem called sin. You may have heard that if you, the parent, just get your act together, everything will be fine, or that if you just stay one step ahead of your kids or become an expert in behavior modification, you will see results. In reality, the roots go much deeper than that, and any long-lasting solutions to family problems must incorporate a more thorough approach.

Our God is a God of order. He created our world with certain laws and principles that, when followed, provide harmony in relationships and success in everyday life. When Adam and Eve sinned, life became more complicated. Disorder and disharmony came into the picture. Every element of life was affected, including the family. Because of sin, relationships experience struggles, unity is threatened, and tension increases. Sin causes people to gravitate toward selfishness, and unchecked selfishness turns into patterns that then become the routines that dictate how a family interacts.

The solution to sin is not rehabilitation; it's salvation. When Christ became our sacrifice, he not only paid the price so that we can have a close relationship with our heavenly Father, but he also offered us an invitation back to orderly relationships. Any true parenting solutions must recognize that the redemptive work of Christ on the cross provides a new way of relating. It's the saving work of God and the power of the Holy Spirit that reintroduces us to balanced relationships. Healthy changes take place on a heart level as we embrace the grace of God.

This may seem to pose a problem for us, as parents, because we mainly discipline in response to behavior, not in response to the heart. We all wish our children would want to choose righteousness, delight in humility, and embrace a life of grace, but they don't. We may pray with and for our kids, have fun family devotion times, and take them to church, but still be met with a bad attitude when we ask for the least bit of cooperation.

So how can we tap into the saving grace of Jesus Christ when we need the trash taken out or the clothes picked up? How is it possible to stay out of the boxing ring—especially when it's become such an ingrained routine? We don't believe that the solution to parental struggles is just to get alone or go to counseling and simply deal with yourself so that you can become more patient or forgiving. Although those solutions are helpful, many times what you need is a strategy to combat your child's selfishness.

THE REALITY OF ANGER

The good news is, you are a part of God's design to change your child's heart. The way you discipline and the routines you develop in family life till the soil for a deeper work of the Holy Spirit in their lives. Your day-to-day parenting can build a framework of character within children so that someday the Spirit of God will breathe life into that framework and create a responsive heart on the deepest level.

One of the flags to help you identify where to start building this framework is the same thing that may be putting you in that boxing ring now—your own anger. Your anger can point out the areas of family life that need work. The family is a classroom, and your anger is often the cue that reveals which part of the curriculum to teach.

Now, we know that some of your anger may be inappropriate, too intense, or just not helpful, so you may need to change *your* heart as well. Parents who find themselves angry a lot tend to feel mixed emotions. On the one hand, they know that being a parent is hard work and sometimes means being the bad guy. On the other hand, they feel guilty about the way they produce results.

Most parents focus on either their anger or how to discipline their children. We believe that one of the most effective ways to make positive changes in family dynamics is to focus on both those things at the same time. You can make adjustments in yourself while at the same time helping your children to make lasting changes in their lives.

A CHANGE OF HEART

We believe that relational routines are more important for a child's heart than most parents realize. In essence, the right kinds of actions set the stage for God to do a deeper work. Parents who take their children to church every week, for instance, and look for ways to make spirituality a positive experience often find that in the midst of that routine, God works to give that child a desire to go to church and grow spiritually. Healthy routines are good for children because they provide them with the vision for what righteousness and godliness look like. How you respond to your son's arguing or bad attitude teaches him important things about life. Furthermore, when you teach your son positive ways of relating to you, you lay the foundation for a healthy spiritual relationship with his heavenly Father. As a parent, you can prepare the way and then pray that God will do the heart work necessary for transformation.

For example, how do your children respond when you give an instruction? Parents must give instructions every day. Your children develop habits of relating to those instructions. Does the cycle that follows your instructions include angry outbursts, grumbling, and bad attitudes on the part of your children and you? God expects children to learn obedience at home, because hidden within that virtue are the principles that will make them successful as they get older. Teaching children to cooperate with you will also help them learn how to obey God and be responsible as they get older.

How do your children respond to correction? If they stomp and pout, you may become angry. Sometimes your anger erupts because they've inconvenienced you, but at other times it surfaces because you can see the danger that lies ahead if this pattern persists. Instead of resorting to harshness and yelling to solve the problem, use anger as a flag to enter into a healthy correction routine. Armed with a specific strategy to implement in a frustrating situation, you'll be less likely to respond to the problem with harshness. Your children will learn to change their hearts, and you will be able to help them make lasting changes. You'll also be preparing them to listen to the corrective words of the Holy Spirit as they grow older. As you take time to examine what happens when instruction or correction takes place in family life, you will begin to see common patterns—predictable routines— in both you and your children. As you become more intentional, you will change the way you relate and begin to develop new routines.

Are bad attitudes a problem in your family? You can probably predict when they will emerge. A bad attitude is often anger in disguise. Children who respond with a bad attitude to instruction or correction demonstrate a heart problem that can't be ignored. Instead of responding to anger with anger, learn a routine to help your children understand why they have a bad attitude and how to change it. If you help them deal with their anger, you will have given them a gift of huge proportions. Children can learn to align their hearts to God by working on their attitudes.

Another common area where routines stand out is when children ask you for something. Parents like to say yes but sometimes must say no. Children usually don't like a no answer and react to it inappropriately with manipulative techniques like arguing, badgering, and whining. If parents get drawn into these negative relating patterns and respond with anger, an unhelpful routine takes place again. When you can identify those destructive relating habits, you can develop a plan for constructive change. Your teaching now will prepare your children to handle the disappointments of life so they can develop a godly contentment as they grow older.

BUT OLD HABITS ARE HARD TO BREAK

Your children need a healthier routine than the boxing ring. Fighting is easy; that's why so many families do it. Discipline can be more difficult. Harshness comes naturally; open dialogue requires more work. Lasting change takes place when parents can show restraint and wisdom. You'll need to discipline, but the way you do so can mean the difference between your child's heart being touched by God or being hardened by hurt and blame.

My (Scott) son Josh heard that we were writing this book and asked to take a look at it in process. I sent him a rough draft of a few chapters, and he liked the concepts he saw. He said, "Dad, after being away at college, I see that some of my friends struggle in areas of their spiritual lives that aren't problems for me. As I think about it, I realize that, in part, that's because of the way you disciplined me as I was growing up." At this point in the conversation, I was feeling pretty good. Then Josh continued. "But I also see some of my friends having some stronger elements of their spiritual lives, and I think you could have done some things differently to prepare me in those areas."

What Josh said was humbling but true. Carrie and I are not perfect parents. If we could do it all over again, we would do some things differently. We're still growing and learning. Josh made another important point. Parents have a tremendous effect on their children's future spiritual lives. Parenting is a walk of faith. Every step of the way you must trust God for solutions and strategies that will bring lasting change for your kids, but the process is a spiritual one for you as well.

Although spiritual instruction may take place during family devotions or in church programs, the most powerful spiritual training is done in the everyday routines of life. In Deuteronomy 6, God outlined a plan for training children. "These commandments that I give you today are to be upon your hearts. Impress them on your children. Talk about them when you sit at home and when you walk along the road, when you lie down and when you get up. Tie them as symbols on your hands and bind them on your foreheads. Write them on the doorframes of your houses and on your gates" (Deuteronomy 6:6-9). When you correct a son for meanness or give directions to your daughter to clean her room, you're teaching more than you realize. The relational routines between you and your children in common tasks prepare them to respond to God. Your home is the training ground for a child's rich spiritual life.

Parenting is an adventure of the greatest sort. It's not enough to simply develop formulas, because children and parents are all different. Families are made up of sinful people; selfishness takes on new and creative forms almost daily. We want to help you see what unhealthy routines your family has developed over the years and to help you look for ways to change those patterns into more productive ones. Our prayer is that as you work through this book you will identify the real issues of life and that the practical day-to-day changes you make will bring lasting results.

PUTTING IT ALL TOGETHER

When You See...
Problem areas in your children or anger in yourself, view them as signals that change is needed. All children have sin natures, and the real work of parenting is to help children connect with the ultimate solution to the problem of sin through a personal work of God in their lives. Your anger may point out a problem in family life and is an indicator that the situation needs attention.

Move into a Routine...

Routines are patterns of behavior, and your family is full of them. Some are good and others need adjustment. Although they are often hidden or taken for granted, you can raise the awareness level so that you can change them into healthier interactions.

Because...

The way you discipline now will influence how your children will respond to life in the future. You are teaching your children how to think about life's challenges. Children will face situations that involve correction, disappointment, temptation, following directions, and bad attitudes for the rest of their lives. You aren't just making family life easier. You are developing routines that will last forever.

QUESTIONS FOR FURTHER DISCUSSION

The questions at the end of each chapter are designed to help you think through the principles of that chapter more thoroughly and provide topics for constructive dialogue. Whether you are reading this book alone, as a couple, with your family, or with a group, use the questions to reflect on the primary issues presented.

"Questions for Further Discussion" are designed to get you talking and reflecting about life. "Digging Deeper" will probe biblical passages to further explore the scriptural roots of the material. "Bringing It Home" provides specific activities for the whole family that will illustrate, teach, and motivate family members of all ages to consider the truths presented in the chapter.

1. What are some things your children do or say that tend to draw you into the boxing ring? What could you do differently in each situation next time?

2. Can you identify some relational routines that exist between you and your children? List a few things you might typically expect when you give your child an instruction or you correct or you give a no answer.

3. What are some common things in your children that make you angry? In what way is your anger an indication of a real problem in them that needs some kind of plan and further work?

DIGGING DEEPER

1. Read 1 Samuel 16:5-7. What principles does God reveal to Samuel while he is looking for a king? Read Matthew 7:15-20. What principle does Jesus reveal about watching out for false teachers? One principle emphasizes external behavior while the other emphasizes the heart. Discuss how the heart and behavior come into play when disciplining children.

2. Here's a quote from this chapter: "Although spiritual instruction may take place during family devotions or in church programs, the most powerful spiritual training is done in the everyday routines of life." Read Deuteronomy 6:6-9. Several opportunities to teach children are mentioned. What are some ways you can use unstructured times to teach about life?

3. Read the two Bible stories in 2 Samuel 16:5-12 and 1 Samuel 26:6-11. In each of these stories the person reacted out of emotion, but David showed restraint and wisdom. Although parents may not respond as violently as the men in the story, how are these situations similar to the way parents feel at times? What kinds of feelings do parents sometimes face?

4. Read Galatians 5:22-23. Which fruit of the Spirit do you find most helpful for you when you work with your children? Which one do you wish your children possessed more of? What can you do to help develop it?

BRINGING IT HOME

Look up the word "routine" in the dictionary. List several good routines or habits in your family that make your home unique and special. Think through areas like travel, entertainment, meal times, and fun times. Emphasize the positive side of routines that you are already enjoying. Do any negative routines come to mind? Don't spend too much time dwelling on the negative, but recognize that you may see some things you'd like to change as you continue to study this book.

2

In your anger do not sin.

EPHESIANS 4:26

"I Hate to Get Angry!"

The Positive Side of Anger

Dear Scott and Joanne,

I used to feel so guilty about my anger. Even when I didn't explode at my kids, I felt bad because of how I felt. In fact, I felt bad anytime I experienced a negative emotion. I used to feel angry about being angry, guilty about feeling guilty, or depressed because I was depressed. This only complicated my problems as I tried to work with my husband and three kids. So then I developed a goal to be less emotional and to somehow turn off my feelings. They were just making my life worse.

Your perspective on emotions has changed the way I think. It never occurred to me to use emotions in a positive way. I always viewed them as weaknesses. I'm still working on my anger, but I feel so much better about the process. God has used your teaching to help me think rightly about my anger and other emotions.

It's so freeing. Now I can be more productive and work with my children in healthier ways.

The interesting thing, though, is that now I'm having more success at helping my nine-year-old son deal with his emotions. He gets mad a lot. I've tried to teach him about the benefit of emotions, and he's responding. Understanding emotions is a key that has opened an important door for my family and for me.

—Joanie from New York City, New York

When Eric came into our office for counseling, he was only seven years old. Already his explosive anger was creating problems in his family. When we talked with Eric, he said, "That's just the way I am. There's nothing I can do." He had already given up hope of ever gaining control of his anger. Eric also felt guilty and ashamed about who he was. One of the first things we said to him was, "You know, Eric, anger is good." He looked at us as if to say, "Who are these crazy people that my parents brought me to see?" We continued by saying, "Anger is good for identifying problems but not good for solving them."

As we worked with Eric, he began to experience hope. Over time, Eric not only gained control of his anger, but he also began to feel better about himself as he discovered how to use emotions to his advantage. His anger became less intense, he was angry less often, and when he did get angry, he knew what to do about it. We told Eric that we didn't just want him to deal with his own anger but we also wanted him to have the tools necessary to help others with their anger. Our goal, we explained, was to teach him how to be a peacemaker, seeing conflict and anger in others and knowing how to bring peace into the situation.

Many parents are like Eric. They've given up hope, believing that they have lost the battle with anger. They're plagued with guilt about their emotions. Before you can improve your anger management or your children's, you must first think rightly about anger. This chapter gives you four truths about emotions in general and ties each one to anger specifically to help you understand what anger is and how it can be useful.

Truth 1: Emotions Are Part of God's Creation

When Adam sinned, sin entered the world, and several consequences followed. Weeds now complicate gardening, women experience pain in childbirth, and relationships are less open because we have a tendency to cover up our true selves. Some people treat emotions as if they are consequences of the Fall instead of parts of God's creation. This misunderstanding leads some to believe that negative emotions such as anger are sinful. These people feel guilty when they get angry and miss the benefits that emotions provide.

A more appropriate view is that emotions are a result of creation, not of the Fall, and that God gave us emotions to be managed and used for his glory. God created us in his image, and he, himself, is often described in Scripture as having emotions. Now, God is God and by definition isn't limited to human traits and feelings, but the very fact that he is described in those terms communicates a common bond that we share with our Creator. Of course, when we experience emotions, our hearts always have a mixture of impurity in them. Because God is holy, his expression of emotion is always righteous and pure. So the similarities between man and God end at his infinite character. The fact remains, however, that anger and other emotions are parts of the raw material in our being. Emotions add zest and passion to what might otherwise be a mundane existence. Life would be monotone without the inflections they bring.

This doesn't mean that the expression of those emotions or their frequency or intensity in our daily lives is always appropriate. Because of our tendency to sin, we sometimes take God's good gifts and misuse them. The Fall tainted emotions in that they can be used in a negative way. But the first step toward making the most of our emotions is to recognize that God has given them to us for a purpose, and we are called to use them in line with that purpose.

Instead of assuming that anger is evil, for instance, we must view it as a misused asset and learn how to utilize it according to its design. Scripture doesn't condemn anger but encourages its control. James 1:19 says "be…slow to become angry." Ephesians 4:26 says, "In your anger do not sin." Neither of these verses condemns anger outright. They call us to moderation.

John, a father of two girls, found this truth to be pivotal in his understanding. "I get angry a lot with my daughters. Their silliness,

---

To start gaining control of your anger, first acknowledge that it is a gift from God, and begin viewing it in a positive way. Some of the other truths about emotion may help you do that.

Jesus was perfect, yet he experienced emotions:

Anxiety: Matthew 26:38-39
Grief: John 11:35
Sadness: Luke 19:41-42
Joy: John 15:11
Compassion: Mark 1:41
Love: John 14:31
Anger: Mark 3:1-5
Peace: John 14:27

meanness, and bad attitudes are high on the list of things that provoke me. I used to feel like I was a bad parent because I got angry with my kids. Now I realize that anger is part of God's plan—I just need to view and manage it differently. Since I've been learning to use anger in a much more positive way, I feel I'm a better dad. I'm relating differently now to my girls, and I know they appreciate the changes they've seen in me."

TRUTH 2: EMOTIONS ARE COMPLEX TOOLS FOR COMMUNICATING

Emotions are a multifaceted part of our everyday lives. Those who study them try to bring order to the picture by identifying several basic emotions that all people experience. For example, Figure 1 identifies nine basic emotions. (Researchers disagree on the number of basic emotions, but most will identify these nine.) They include feelings of sadness, anger, joy, disgust, fear, guilt, anticipation, surprise, and hopelessness. Each of these emotions has degrees of intensity that result in varying feelings. For instance, fear may start as apprehension and then move to terror. Surprise may change from a mere distraction to an intense amazement.

Combining different emotions creates a library of feelings, further complicating the emotional picture. Fear and surprise join to create alarm. Joy and anticipation together give a sense of excitement. Sadness and anger produce sullenness. Fear mixed with anticipation results in anxiety.

As you can see, emotions can get complex very quickly. It's no wonder so many people are not only confused but may even give up trying to understand them at all. They just determine to ignore the discussion and take life as it comes. These people have little control of their emotional responses and miss much of the benefit that reflection provides. They often view emotions as enemies to be fought or geysers to be stopped up. But why work against the way God created you when you can work with those feelings and enjoy life more fully? Instead of viewing emotions as things that just happen to you, learn to use them as tools as you interact with others.

One mom said, "I'm just beginning to understand the complexity of my emotions. I feel a lot of things and tend to react without thinking. It's as if the emotions have the ability to bypass my brain. It takes work to understand what's actually going on. I'm learning to slow down and think more about what I'm feeling. I'm making progress and I actually feel as if I'm gaining some insight into how I relate to my kids. They're seeing some changes in me too. I'm becoming less afraid of emotions and more eager to understand them and make the most of them in our family."

Solemn	→**Sadness**	→ Grief
Irritated	→**Anger**	→ Rage
Encouraged	→**Joy**	→ Possessiveness
Bored	→**Disgust**	→ Hate
Apprehensive	→**Fear**	→ Terror
Mistaken	→**Guilt**	→ Failure
Curious	→**Anticipation**	→ Obsession
Distracted	→**Surprise**	→ Amazement
Apathetic	→**Hopelessness**	→ Despair

Figure 1: Intensity Levels for Basic Emotions

When parents choose to reflect only anger, they limit themselves dramatically. Families benefit when they experiment with other emotional options as well. Marilyn surprised her eight-year-old son after he put his feet on the table during dinner. She felt angry, but she chose to respond differently. "Do you know what the Bible says about beautiful feet?" she asked in a playful tone.

Expecting a harsh response the boy was shocked by his mother's question and curious about the answer. "No," he replied with question in his voice.

"The Bible says, 'Beautiful are the feet of those who bring good news.' Now I have some good news for you. Dessert is served only to those whose feet are under the table." Marilyn made her point, and she didn't have to use anger to do it. During dessert, several minutes after the previous incident, she made a passing request, "Please don't put your feet on this table."

Her son responded, "Okay."

This mom avoided what could have been an ugly scene by exercising some restraint on her anger and responding in a wise way. By stopping each time you get angry and evaluating the situation, you can use anger to point out problems and then choose another strategy for your response.

The complexity of emotions requires that we learn how to manage them, not just react. Anger, just one of the emotions given to us by God, can be confusing. Suppressing anger often results in physical problems and is actually a way to turn anger against oneself. But some people believe the only way to deal with anger is to drain it by venting. In fact, common advice from some psychologists suggests that anger must somehow be released. They say that you have the right to yell, scream, kick, and throw a tantrum because anger is an energy smoldering deep inside that needs to be expressed. We don't believe that repressing emotions is good, but that doesn't mean venting them is helpful either. When people feel the freedom to vent anger, they end up hurting others and damaging relationships.

The Bible takes a different approach. Proverbs 29:11 says, "A fool gives full vent to his anger, but a wise man keeps himself under control." Control is better than venting. Control allows us to use anger as a tool rather than a weapon. When parents and children recognize the complexity of emotions and how to wisely choose which emotion to use in a particular situation, they will feel anger less intensely and less often.

TRUTH 3: EMOTIONS GIVE US SIGNALS

Emotions are not just for ambiance or atmosphere. They also have a very practical purpose—they reveal things about life. Emotions are like a "sixth sense," helping us recognize things about our environment. It's amazing how many times a day a person feels information before the mind is aware of it. You feel like someone is watching you, like something's wrong, like you're on the wrong road, or that this is going to be a good day. Those who are sensitive to their emotions have the added advantage of picking up signals that others might miss.

One mom told the story of how she discovered that her three-year-old had eaten a bottle of baby aspirin. "I walked into the living room where my son was playing on the floor and sensed something wasn't right. I asked him what he was doing, and his answer just wasn't what I expected. Instead of going on about my business, I decided to sit with him a minute. It was then that I smelled his breath and knew something was up. I looked over at the table and saw the empty bottle. I scooped him up and raced to the emergency room. I'm still not sure what the first clue was, but I know that I sensed something first."

A salesman knows when it's just the right time to close the deal. A husband is amazed at his wife's perceptiveness to sense a problem in their son. A teacher decides to let the class take a stretch break. If you were to ask those people how they knew how to respond to each situation, they might not be able to articulate what it was that gave them the clue. They just felt as if it was the right thing to do.

If you analyze the previously described situations, you will discover that each involved specific objective signals that don't have to do with emotions. People relied on details that they saw, heard, or remembered. However, those cues triggered emotional responses, not intellectual reason. Salesmen, teachers, and parents learn to look for signals and clues in others in the form of expressions or behavior. But some of the best skill comes from an emotional sense that this is the right thing at the right time.

Imagine a car's control panel with many little lights. They flash occasionally, sometimes even intensely. With experience, you begin to learn about all those lights and what they mean. One indicates it's time to add oil, another reveals that the trunk is open. Yet another tells you that it's time to take the car in for maintenance. Emotions are like those little lights. It takes time to understand what they mean and how to respond rightly to them. When you become more in touch with the emotional signals in relationships and are more sensitive to others, you can begin to respond in healthier ways.

Hundreds of times a day, you make decisions about life. You'd be surprised how many times it's a minor emotional signal that gets you started. Feeling apprehensive about the weather may motivate you to turn on the radio to get an update. Boredom may stimulate you to be creative about dinner plans. Your child may make a sarcastic remark after just a minor irritation. In each case, a small emotional signal motivated the action.

Considering emotional cues may seem contradictory to what you've heard in the past. We've all been warned, "Be careful about making decisions based on emotions." That's good advice, especially as you're growing in your experience, because emotions can give unclear signals about life situations. It would be unwise to leave the house messy just because you don't feel like cleaning it, or confront someone just because he made you mad. That's not what we're talking about here. When a decision is very important, it's essential to base it on more than a hunch or an emotional cue.

Emotions need to be interpreted wisely. For example, you may use the emotion of guilt as a motivation to evaluate yourself and repent of sin. That would be a healthy response to something you've done wrong. On the other hand, if your guilt feelings are misplaced, you might feel unwarranted shame. For instance, societal pressure may make you feel guilty that you're staying at home with your children instead of working for pay, or going out to work and leaving your children with others. If you are aware of the dangers of misinterpreting emotions, you will realize that outside pressure is creating a false sense of guilt. You can then develop a determination to withstand the manipulative techniques that others might use. The emotion of guilt provided the clue that you needed to do some evaluating.

Understanding emotions and doing some healthy self-reflection can turn feelings into assets in daily life. Anger, for instance, is a flag that says, "Something's wrong here, and I need to do something about it." The anger does not define what is wrong. You need to take time to think and interpret anger's signal appropriately before you take action.

Sometimes the problem is outside you, such as when your son leaves his bike in the driveway, one brother hits another, or a teenager leaves a sticky mess on the counter. But often the problem has something to do with an internal issue such as an unrealistic expectation that your two-year-old can clean up the toys alone, a selfishness in a mom's heart when she's planned too much into her schedule, or an overambitious desire to have a clean house while managing three children under the age of five.

One dad told us, "I like this idea that anger has a good side, but I feel bad when I get angry. I don't like anger, and I wish I could respond differently." We believe that the key to using anger in a productive way is to separate the trigger from the response. If you can use anger to identify problems but not to react to them, your perspective on anger will change. You will begin to see anger and all emotions as signals that can help you know how to respond to others more effectively.

Too often people move to the solution before evaluation and then use anger to manipulate others or the situation. When we use anger to help us know when something is wrong, we can benefit from its signals without falling into its dangers.

TRUTH 4: EMOTIONS AFFECT ENERGY LEVELS

Some emotions, such as fear or frustration, increase your energy level, whereas other feelings, like sadness or hopelessness, decrease your energy. Both groups of emotions have God-ordained purposes. When you take advantage of these signals, you gain the most from your emotions. Feelings often motivate us to action or inaction. Fear, for instance, provides extra energy for an exhausted parent to get off the porch and rescue a two-year-old who's headed for the street. Gratefulness motivates one to send a card of appreciation. Sadness or grief might force us to step back and let go of something after we experience a loss.

Anger is an emotion that increases energy. When you get angry, several things happen inside your body all at the same time. Your heart rate, blood pressure, and rate of breathing increase. Blood sugar levels rise, your pupils dilate, and your muscles become tense. Your adrenal glands release adrenaline, and your awareness intensifies. All of these reactions are designed by God to prepare you to fight an actual physical threat or run from it. You may not be faced with imminent danger, but a physical response occurs in your body when your children threaten your peace or traffic challenges your tight schedule.

The increased energy that anger gives has both a positive and a negative side. When you're angry, you're more motivated to solve problems, confront offenders, or make a change in your life. It's *how* you make changes, however, that determines the final result in relationships. It's here that you may need to learn new skills for problem solving, new strategies for confrontation, and healthy ways of communicating your concerns.

The increase in energy that anger produces is sometimes described as a boiling pot about to blow its top. Physical acts of violence such as slamming the door, stomping, hitting, grabbing, and pushing are common ways to release steam. Those who have learned to control their physical responses, though, often struggle with their mouths.

It's a lifestyle of anger that the Scriptures condemn:

- Do not make friends with a hot-tempered man, do not associate with one easily angered, or you may learn his ways and get yourself ensnared. (Proverbs 22:24-25)
- An angry man stirs up dissension, and a hot-tempered one commits many sins. (Proverbs 29:22)
- Get rid of all bitterness, rage and anger, brawling and slander, along with every form of malice. (Ephesians 4:31)
- But now you must rid yourselves of all such things as these: anger, rage, malice, slander, and filthy language from your lips. (Colossians 3:8)
- Man's anger does not bring about the righteous life that God desires. (James 1:20)

Their words, volume, or tone of voice may be even more destructive than physical displays of anger. Even those who have learned to control their mouths will sometimes resort to more sophisticated ways of communicating their anger—giving someone the silent treatment or the glare we call the "hairy eyeball." The angry mom may send "Morse Code" messages to the whole family by the way she shuts the refrigerator just a little harder, pushes chairs around, grunts, sighs, and clangs the pots on the stove. No violence, no mean words, but everyone knows Mom is angry. The atmosphere is thick, and the air is tense.

Some people rely on anger to get things done. The rush of energy that anger provides becomes the fuel to keep them going during the day. If they can get angry about something, they can remain productive. If things settle down, they are less motivated. These people may even generate conflict to increase anger levels in order to get themselves moving. They become addicted to anger's energy. One young man told us, "I like to get angry. I get more done, and I have the courage to confront problems and accomplish things." Anger does have the power to motivate. Unfortunately, this young man relied on anger too much. In time, he became addicted to anger; it had adverse effects on his family and made him anxious and high-strung.

Long-term anger damages our bodies as well as our relationships with others. As a parent, instead of holding on to anger or trying to foster it, use the extra energy that anger provides to identify problems in your children and move you into a new routine that will help your kids build character.

ANGER'S MESSAGE

Understanding these four truths about emotions can help you take advantage of your anger and use it productively. Anger has a specific job. It gives the message that something is wrong. That wrong can be internal or external or both. Bickering, defiance, or a bad attitude in your kids may spark your anger (external). Or the anger may come from your unrealistic expectations, demandingness, or holding on to a right that needs to be sacrificed (internal). Anger only alerts you to a problem. You then must figure out what the real issues are.

A helpful way to uncover what is behind your anger is to recognize anger's five basic causes. These five causes overlap at points, and you may find that the situation you're experiencing fits more than one, but this list is often helpful to bring some rationale to feelings. Use these causes to guide your self-reflection when you start to feel angry.

What Is Rage?

When anger becomes intense, it's called rage, or anger out of control. The person experiencing rage can no longer think clearly. He's lost the ability to evaluate or consider the situation. Now, he's just reacting and functioning on raw emotion. For some, this means blowing up, ranting, and raving. For others, rage leads to shutting down and refusing to talk.

In both cases, rage prevents clear thinking and keeps a person from evaluating the situation objectively. Use rage as a signal that you need to take a break and settle down so that you can approach the problem in a healthier way. One way that you know you're ready to move on is that you can identify what is fueling your anger.

Physical Pain

At the heart of all anger is pain. When a person stubs his toe or bumps his head on a pipe in the basement, anger is often the immediate response. When a child hits you or you step on a sharp toy, your anger may, in part, be fueled by the physical pain you experience.

Blocked Goals

Trying to leave the house by 7:35 A.M. and turning to see that your three-year-old took her coat off again may cause you to feel angry because of a blocked goal. Getting out to the main road and finding that traffic will make you late may also cause angry feelings because your goal of arriving at your appointment on time is blocked. Trying to finish a project with an uncooperative child or looking for a misplaced shoe for the third time that day when you need to get ready for company is frustrating and can lead to anger.

Violated Rights

When her five-year-old is knocking on the bathroom door, a mom may feel angry and think, "I have the right to go to the bathroom in peace." A dad may believe that he has a right to come home and have a few minutes to relax in quiet before taking on family problems. In each of these cases, parents may feel that a child has violated their rights and may react with anger.

Unfairness

When a mom sees a big brother picking on his sister, or a younger child harassing an older one, she may get angry because of the obvious unfairness of the situation. A dad may feel it's unfair that he has to help bathe the kids after putting in a hard day's work. When parents perceive life to be unfair for them or for their family, they often experience anger.

Unmet Expectations

Life might be rather predictable if it weren't for children. A mom might say, "I expected to arrive home from work to cook dinner, but instead I come home to this mess." Unmet expectations seem to go along with the job of parenting and often result in angry feelings.

Understanding the five causes of anger can help you as you relate to your family. Each time you feel angry, stop for a minute and try to identify which of these is the cause. Putting a label on your feelings may help you redirect some of that energy to a more productive response. You may begin to see patterns in yourself and identify one particular cause that is more common for you. This observation can help you know how to adjust your reaction.

ISN'T MY ANGER JUSTIFIED WHEN MY KIDS DO THE WRONG THING?

Some view their anger as justified because they are right and others are wrong. They believe that being right is the only ticket required to launch into an adult tantrum. But saying "He made me angry" implies that external events can determine your emotional intensity. The dad who links the trigger (what made him angry) and response (what he does with his anger) too closely ends up believing that others have made him the way he is. When parents do this, they often blame their kids for problems and rarely take responsibility for their own emotions. In many cases, of course, the child is indeed wrong. It isn't helpful, though, to expect our children to bear the responsibility for our anger in addition to what they did wrong. The mom who says, "I wouldn't have to get angry if my kids would listen the first time," has fallen into the trap of blaming her children for her angry responses.

The truth of the matter is that it doesn't take much character to see something wrong, but it takes wisdom to know how to respond to it. There's a big difference between a button that pops up on a turkey to announce that it's done and a cook who knows how to make a great dinner. Some people are like those little turkey buttons—whenever something goes wrong they pop up with angry reactions and then try to justify abusiveness by claiming they are right.

It's not enough to be right in life; parents also need to be wise. Real wisdom knows how to respond in a way that brings change, not revenge. As parents, we don't just want to punish our kids for doing something wrong; we want to help them change their hearts. Anger may reveal what's wrong, but it's rarely a good solution to a problem. Once you identify an offense, it's best to consider how to motivate change.

SPIRIT-FILLED FEELINGS

Galatians 5:22-23 provides a list of the fruit of the Spirit. Interestingly enough, the first three are often considered emotions: love, joy, and peace. When we obey God and allow him to direct our lives, we can experience God-filled emotions. Jeanette, a mother of four, said, "I'm learning to respond differently to my anger. In fact, it's freeing to not feel like I have to engage in every argument that comes up in my home. I'm able to move above the bickering and petty discussions to a more mature response. I know that prayer and hard work are paying off because I'm enjoying a greater peace in my home. There are still problems, but I don't get sucked into the old patterns anymore, and I'm able to help my family because I'm staying calm." We believe that Jeanette is experiencing a feeling of peace as the spiritual consequence of trusting God in the midst of conflict.

The idea of separating the signal (something is wrong) from the response (solving the problem) is refreshing for many. No longer can a parent say, "My harshness is justified because of my son's defiance." The two are not necessarily linked. Yes, the child is wrong and anger may have helped reveal the problem, but that doesn't justify harsh words or actions.

Parents usually set the emotional climate in a family, and children learn to ride the waves that are set in motion. When parents learn to live life more calmly, children see that and follow the leader. The way you respond to conflict, anger, and the challenges of family life can bring a wave of peace into your home. But the benefits don't just come in family life; they come in your heart as well. The Holy Spirit wants to do a work in you. Many times he uses the choices you make in everyday life to stimulate godly feelings. It's just another benefit of following God's ways to live.

Remember Eric, that seven-year-old boy who struggled with anger? Eric is fourteen now and a much more peaceable boy. He looks at angry outbursts as part of his past and is much more at ease in frustrating circumstances. He now helps others deal with their anger, using some of the things he's learned over the last few years.

You may have been told that your anger is a problem. You may have even read books on anger that teach you how to become less angry by changing yourself. But changing yourself can be hard when you know that many of the things you get mad at are real problems in your kids. You've known all along that your anger is provoked at least in part by other people's actions. You realize you don't just need to change you; you need help in changing others. We know that too. We want to help you make adjustments in the way you relate so that your children will change and you will become less explosive.

In order to take advantage of routines for developing character, you must first learn to use your frustration as an asset. Review the four truths mentioned in this chapter. Write them down and post them in various places. Learn to recognize your anger and stop the progression to hurtful responses. Begin to use anger to help you make the necessary changes in your family. Take some time to pray for God's help as you learn to use your emotions, and anger in particular, for benefit in your family.

You will be amazed at the results.

PUTTING IT ALL TOGETHER

When You See...
Emotions in yourself and others, view them as assets to be managed instead of liabilities to be eliminated. Anger points out that something is wrong and needs attention.

Move into a Routine...
Before you react with anger, consider a wise way to respond. Separate the trigger of anger from the response. Wisdom often results from thoughtful reflection. Your choice to respond in a more gentle or creative way may be just the thing that helps a person change.

Because...
Anger is good for identifying problems but not good for solving them. God created us as emotional beings, and those emotions provide insight into life.

QUESTIONS FOR FURTHER DISCUSSION

1. List five pet peeves you have around your house. A pet peeve is something that tends to make you angry. What problem is identified by each of these triggers?

2. Look at the chart in Figure 1 on page 21. Identify one set of emotions and describe a time in your life when the intensity level increased through the various stages.

3. Look at James 1:19. People use a number of techniques to prevent themselves from reacting in anger, such as counting to ten. Many of those techniques involve statements people make to themselves. Share some of the things you say to yourself to help you slow down your anger and prevent you from exploding.

DIGGING DEEPER

1. Look at the six types of anger mentioned in Ephesians 4:31. How would you define these different types of anger and distinguish them from each other?

2. Read Galatians 5:22-23 and talk about the idea of Spirit-filled feelings. How can you get them, and how do they help you relate better to your children?

3. Read Ephesians 4:26-27. What ways might the devil gain a foothold in a person's or family's life through anger?

4. Read Genesis 4:4-7. Using the causes of anger mentioned in this chapter, identify which ones may have been factors in Cain's predicament. What does it mean, "If you do not do what is right, sin is crouching at your door; it desires to have you, but you must master it" (verse 7)?

BRINGING IT HOME

Taking each of the emotions in the center column of Figure 1, go around the family and fill in the blank. "One thing that makes me feel [emotion] is ———." This can be funny and informative as family members share about things that make them feel a particular way.

3

Listen to advice and accept instruction,
and in the end you will be wise.

PROVERBS 19:20

"They Don't Do What I Say"

Instruction:
Giving the Gift of Responsibility

Dear Scott and Joanne,

I was so discouraged. I can't believe all the things I do for my family. I pick up after my kids, shop, cook, clean, drive kids here and there, keep everyone organized—it never seems to stop. I knew that my two boys, ages nine and seven, could help me, but they didn't and I stopped trying. Every time I asked one of them to do something I got an argument or a bad attitude. It just wasn't worth it. It was easier to do the work myself. Then I began to realize what I was doing to the boys. By avoiding the struggle, I was missing a valuable opportunity for training.

Now, I've learned a process for giving instructions that has given me what I need. It has helped me see where my boys must change. I know that in the process I'm teaching them about life. Most importantly, I'm preparing the way for them to follow God's instructions. I'm more motivated now to take the extra time and energy because I know I'm not just running a household, I'm working with the Lord to build character in my sons.

—Carla from Providence, Rhode Island

Parents give instructions. It's part of the job. What seems like hundreds of times a day, we tell our children what, when, and how to do things. We all wish kids would see what needs to be done and do it, but that isn't reality in most homes. Children leave shoes by the door, drop their backpacks in the kitchen, watch the trash overflow, seem content to live in a messy room, leave bikes out on the front lawn, and the list goes on and on.

Trying to direct family life can be a huge job. As one mom told us, "I can't believe I've got to organize someone else's life. I'm having enough trouble with my own!" As family size increases, getting everything done often becomes a matter of precision and clockwork, further setting families up for emotional intensity. Larger families are a blessing but demand a more rigorous system for staying on top of things. (The dad who said, "I never missed one of my son's ball games as he was growing up," surely didn't have more than one child.) Giving instructions is not just a matter of convenience—it's survival!

The word "instruction" comes from the words "in" and "structure" and basically means "to put structure into." When someone comes on the scene and gives instructions, that person brings structure to the situation and helps people know what to do. Mom sees the need to clean up around the house or get things going to meet a deadline and begins giving instructions to move the family in a positive direction. She adds the structure needed at the moment to make family life work. Unfortunately, because of the well-worn relationship between parent and child, kids often react with resistance. At that point parents often become more intense in their instruction or just give up. What was meant to be a move toward order and structure can turn relationships into chaos.

Sometimes parents can't tell whether children are being unresponsive because of developmental issues, because they didn't understand the instruction, or because they're just tired. An instruction routine gives parents a tool to draw a line between those issues and problems like disobedience, defiance, or a bad attitude. The routine presented in this chapter will slow down the instruction process so that you can determine whether a child is resisting your leadership or just can't handle the situation at the moment. It also breaks down the work of giving and following instructions into smaller pieces that both children and parents can accept without feeling frustrated.

There's more to giving instructions than just accomplishing tasks or getting children to do what parents say for the sake of convenience. Valuable lessons for life are hidden within the instruction process. Through instruction, children learn character and skills that will help them to be successful outside the home. They learn things like how to set aside their agenda for someone else, how to complete a job without Mom or Dad's reminding them, how to report back when they're done, and how to be responsible when no one is watching.

Most importantly, children learn to obey Mom and Dad so that they will have the necessary character to obey God as they grow older. Maybe that's why Solomon speaks fifteen times in the book of Proverbs about the importance of listening to instructions. As you concentrate on a routine for giving instructions, you will pave the way for healthy spiritual relationships between your children and God. By teaching children to follow directions you help them develop the character they need to listen to God's instructions and obey him. It's a lot of work, but the time you invest now has benefits that will last a lifetime. After all, as adults, we must often comply with instructions that we don't particularly like. Sometimes God asks us to do something we don't fully understand or wish we didn't have to do. Obedience usually requires work, self-discipline, and humility.

The instruction process builds character by helping children learn to follow directions without arguing or complaining. When parents give up on giving instructions, they miss valuable teaching opportunities. That doesn't mean parents should just overpower their kids. If you work to implement an instruction routine, both you and your kids will benefit. You will not only learn how to teach your children to follow directions, but you will also teach them a godly response to instruction. The ramifications are important because as you do the daily work of parenting, your children are learning how to respond not only to you but also to their future employers, team leaders, and ultimately to God.

The book of Proverbs emphasizes the value of listening to instructions:

- Listen, my sons, to a father's instruction; pay attention and gain understanding. (4:1)
- Hold on to instruction, do not let it go; guard it well, for it is your life. (4:13)
- Listen to my instruction and be wise; do not ignore it. (8:33)
- Instruct a wise man and he will be wiser still; teach a righteous man and he will add to his learning. (9:9)
- Listen to advice and accept instruction, and in the end you will be wise. (19:20)

THE BATTLE

Many parents feel that giving instructions is like being in a battle with continual conflict and no rest. When children resist, parents often resort to yelling in order to accomplish just about anything.

Take Allison for example, a single mom who stops at the store on her way home from work. She walks in the door to find her ten-year-old son, Sean, watching television. "Sean, would you please help me bring in the groceries from the car?"

On her second trip into the house she sees that he's still watching television. "SEAN! Turn off the TV and help me."

On her third trip, Sean has his hand on the television knob, watching one more glimpse of the show. "Sean! Turn that TV off right now and get out to that car and bring in those bags."

Sean grunts and turns it off.

As Mom brings in the next load, Sean has disappeared. She yells, "Seeaaan!"

Sean yells from upstairs, "I can't find my shoes."

Mom yells, "Go out and get that last bag without your shoes!"

Then comes round two. When Sean comes in with the last bag, Mom begins another instruction by saying, "Sean, please put away the toilet paper in the bathroom."

Sean says, "Why do I have to..."

That's all Mom needs to set off the explosion. She starts yelling at her son about all the things she does and he doesn't do and so on.

If you were to ask Allison about this problem, she would say, "This happens all the time. It's not just a one-time problem." The reality is that many families have developed a similar negative routine. Over time this pattern becomes the normal way of relating in family life. With each cycle, Mom's intensity increases and Sean becomes less and less responsive. The pattern often looks like Figure 2.

As this cycle continues, frustration mounts, resistance increases, and the result is a distant and tense relationship between the parent and child.

It's time to break this destructive cycle. It's easy to feel angry because your children aren't doing what you say. At those moments, don't respond with more harshness. Instead, move into a routine that teaches your kids how to accept instructions in life. This new pattern not only makes family life easier, but each step will train your children to respond to other leaders and eventually to God's instruction.

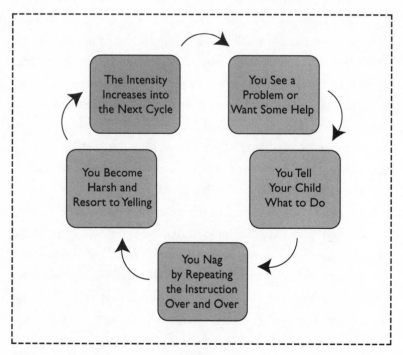

Figure 2: A Frustrating Instruction Cycle

Step 1: Get Close Together →
The Child Comes When Called

Many parents see a problem and start giving instructions immediately. This often means that they yell across the parking lot or bark commands from the other side of the house. We believe this approach isn't the best. It's not enough to see the need and tell someone to respond to it. That approach doesn't demonstrate value for the relationship. Parenting isn't just about getting tasks done; it's about building relationships at the same time.

Start by getting close to your child. Most of the time this means that before you give an instruction you call your child over to you. This presents a problem in many young families because preschoolers often don't come when they're called. The fact is, even older children don't come when they're called unless they are taught to do so.

When I (Scott) wanted to teach Megan and Elizabeth to come when they're called, they were four years old. Because we adopted these girls into our family, they spent their first few years following other rules or patterns in relationships. Carrie and I told them, "In our home we have a Come When You're Called Rule." We explained that this rule simply means that when we call your name, you come to within a few feet and say, "What Dad?" or "What Mom?"

Although the kids agreed in theory, practice was a little difficult at first. If our girls were playing in the backyard, I would come to the back door and say, "Megan," only to hear, "What?" I would then say, "Remember, you need to come when I call." She would, sometimes reluctantly, get up and come over to hear what I had to say. When she came I would respond in different ways. Sometimes I would just say, "I want to tell you that I love you," and we would enjoy a giggling time together. Other times I would say, "I have a snack here for you."

Still other times I would instruct or correct. The girls never knew what I wanted. They just knew that when I called their names they needed to come. We talked about Samuel in the Bible who heard his name called in the night. Instead of yelling across the house, Samuel went to Eli to see what he wanted. Eli, realizing that it must be the Lord calling, told Samuel to answer with a willingness to listen and respond. We're asking our kids to do the same thing.

Parents often ask, "What do I do in the grocery store when I call my preschooler and he runs away?" Well, the grocery store isn't the place to practice. That's the final exam! By practicing over and over at home and at the park, children learn to respond in public. It takes lots of work to develop new routines. Choose times and places that are convenient for you so that you don't have the added frustration of a tight schedule or a potentially embarrassing situation.

Like every step in a good instruction routine, getting close to each other requires changes from both child and parent. Children also find it tempting to yell across the house. Now children learn that dialogue only takes place when relationship has been established through eye contact and proximity. Sometimes it's the small things that demonstrate a parent cares or that a child is willing to listen. Putting down the paper, looking up from the computer, or just turning to face your child before you speak communicates the importance of what you are about to say. Rather than competing with headphones, a mom asks her son to not only turn off the CD player but also take off the headphones to demonstrate a willingness to listen.

Being physically close before talking communicates that the coming instruction is important. In an office, an instruction has more weight if the boss takes the time to come over to the assistant's desk to talk instead of giving the instruction from across the room. The same thing is true at home. With a particularly overactive child, sometimes it's helpful to gently hold both hands and look into his eyes while you're talking. This further emphasizes the importance of the relationship, not just the instruction.

Some parents report major improvement in a child's responsiveness when they begin to implement this step and give instructions only when the child is within a few feet. Notice the difference in these two examples of a dad and his twelve-year-old son, Mark:

Option 1: Dad sees that his son is awake and yells down the hall, "Mark, don't forget to take the trash out this morning." Mark grunts and rolls his eyes.

Option 2: Dad walks down the hall to Mark's bedroom. "Good morning, Mark, how are you doing?"

"Okay."

"How did you sleep?"

"I woke up a lot for some reason, but I feel okay now."

"Did you see our team won last night?"

"No, what happened?"

"They pulled the pitcher and put in their closer. He really did the job."

"That's great."

"Hey Mark, today is Saturday, and the trash gets picked up. Could you please get those cans out to the street?"

"Yeah, okay."

When a parent and child move close before talking, they're likely to stop what they're doing in order to have a conversation. Their concentration is interrupted, and this prepares both of them to focus on something new.

Closeness also allows you to see how your child is doing before you launch into your instruction. You may even change your approach or postpone the instruction based on what you learn when you get close. For example, a dad may want to give an instruction, but when he gets close, he sees that his daughter is doing her homework. Dad then decides to postpone the instruction instead of interrupting her.

Being close is especially important when relating to teenagers. Teens need relationship and a sense of value tied closely to the instruction process. In fact, the stronger the relationship is, the less likely it is that you'll get resistance. Sometimes young people resent having to share in the workload of running a household. You might hear them say something like, "My parents are always ordering me around. It's like I'm their slave." When parents take time to show value for the relationship before giving instructions, they can build a sense of teamwork with their teens.

When children can't see how *instruction* is related to *relationship*, they are more likely to justify unkind words or dishonoring actions when they don't like what you've told them to do. They don't understand that obedience is a demonstration of love. Getting physically close makes a statement about who we are together. Face-to-face contact says, "I care about you." Eye contact communicates value.

Children need to learn how to come when called, but in some situations the most loving thing is for you to go to them. Sometimes you may want to take the extra energy to stop what you're doing and walk over to your child before giving an instruction. You're saying, "I value you enough to come into your world before telling you to do something." This also teaches children to value the person, not just accomplish a task. As a parent, you need to decide in each situation if you will go to your child or ask your child to come to you. Both ways of relating are important.

By affirming your relationship in the midst of the instruction, you teach your children an important lesson about the way God relates to us. Spirituality isn't just a list of dos and don'ts, but it comes within the sphere of relationship. Alex, a father of three, says it well, "I had a picture in my mind of a Father who yells instructions down from heaven. Distance and harshness characterized my view of God. It wasn't until I became a dad and remembered how my parents treated me that I began to see the connection. I was viewing God based on what I had learned in my family growing up. I work hard now to give instructions in a more relational manner. It's amazing how something as simple as giving and receiving instructions can give you a perspective of who God is and how he relates to us."

Over time, children learn that you're not going to engage in dialogue across the house. Either you are going to go to them or expect them to come to you before you begin talking. One mom came into the kitchen to find the counter messy. She determined that her thirteen-year-old daughter, Stephanie, should clean it up. Her inclination was to yell, "Stephanie!" like she usually did, even though she didn't know where her daughter was. Instead, Mom went to find her.

She knocked on Stephanie's door only to hear, "What?"

Instead of giving the instruction, Mom decided to address the way they were relating. "I don't want to talk through a door. Please open it up."

"I'm getting dressed."

"Then please come and see me as soon as you're done."

This mom was determined to break the negative cycle of their usual routine, so she postponed the instruction for a few minutes until the process could go well.

STEP 2: CONSIDER THE TIMING → THE CHILD RESPONDS

Another important step in a good instruction routine is to consider timing. Is it best to address this problem right now or would it be better to talk about it later? No one likes to be ambushed when coming in the door or just getting out of bed in the morning. I (Joanne) enjoy going into my son's bedroom to wake him. I sit on his bed and rub his back a little and tell him gently that it's time to get up. Unfortunately, some mornings I look around his messy room and mentally create an extensive to-do list for him before his eyes are even open. It takes patience and self-control for me to hold my tongue and wait for a more appropriate time to launch into the jobs that he needs to do. Timing is important. I want to let my son wake up to our relationship before I move to instruction.

As parents, we need to see the difference between the issue and the process. The issue is the problem needing an instruction. The process is the way you formulate that instruction. Parents who realize that a child needs an instruction must stop and think of the best way to present it. Ask yourself, "How can I communicate this problem to my child in the most effective way?" Pausing for just a moment, or in some cases, waiting a few hours, may prove to be the most productive way to deal with a problem.

For instance, a dad might say to his son, "Hi Curt, I'm glad you're home," when Curt comes home from school. He engages Curt in dialogue about the day for a few minutes and then says, "After you put your books away and get a snack, would you please come and talk with me? I have a couple of things for you to do." Dad is trying to be sensitive to the timing of his instructions.

Considering the timing can go a long way toward getting a positive response, but more importantly it emphasizes the relationship between parent and child. Giving the instructions is important, but a little preparation says that the child is even more important. It's a small way of saying, "I love you," to a child even in the midst of the work of family life.

Now, you may be thinking, "I've got so much that needs to be done around here, I don't have time to spend figuring out a big strategy for presenting it." Granted, much of the time, giving instructions on the spot gets the job done. If, however, you are experiencing more resistance than you'd like, maybe it's time to take a closer look. It could be that you have been overemphasizing the tasks and underemphasizing the relationship between you and your kids.

One mom said, "Most of the time I just give instructions to Hunter in the course of life and everything works fine, but when I have something that's a little bigger than usual, I consider timing more. I like it when my boss at work gives me a little warning before giving me another job to do. She'll even set an appointment to discuss it. I've tried the same thing at home, and it works great. I'll tell Hunter I'd like to get together with him in a few minutes to talk about something. He comes ready to hear what I have to say. I think the small warning helps him get ready for what's coming."

The way you communicate an instruction is important because it often influences how the child will respond. Yelling breeds more yelling. Irritation encourages defensiveness. When you see a problem, take a moment and ask yourself whether your child is ready to receive an instruction so that the process can go well. A good parenting routine for giving instructions begins before the first words are spoken.

In Step 2, parents take an extra moment to consider timing, but children also have a responsibility. They need to learn to be responsive to parents. Sometimes children build walls so that no time is right to give them instructions. In those situations you shouldn't cower and walk away, but neither should you have to fight. Introducing the conversation with something positive such as, "I'd like to talk with you," may be just that small introduction that says, "I value our relationship," and prevents an explosive interaction.

As you consider timing, you'll want to make different adjustments depending on the age of your child. Young children need to learn obedience, so we may give less warning and expect a prompt response. Older children, and certainly teenagers, need more time to prepare

themselves. Teens will need to adjust their own expectations or agendas. This takes some work for the teen and patience for the parent.

When a child continually demonstrates resistance to instructions,
it's time to decide whether you need to emphasize relationship more
or you need to discipline for a lack of responsiveness. Training is work,
and some children need to learn how to demonstrate genuine responsiveness when someone wants to talk with them. If you ask your son
to come help in the kitchen and before you finish your instruction
he's whining and complaining, then stop the process. You may have
to postpone discipline for a time because you need to get the table set
or food out in order to stay on schedule, but don't just let it go. After
dinner, talk to your son and confront him about his poor attitude.
Explain the importance of cooperation and that you're going to have
him help you with dinner every evening for a while. Increasing the
workload to give more opportunity to practice may be just the constructive consequence needed to build a cooperative attitude.

Sometimes you must ask your children to help right away, and
they need to be able to respond quickly. When you arrive home with
a car full of groceries, you don't have the luxury to consider the timing. You may have to ask children to stop their computer game or take
a break from talking on the phone to help unload the car. When the
relationship is generally strong, however, interruptions are easier for
children to accept.

When you factor in the timing of instructions, you don't do things
the same way anymore. New routines take the place of old habits.
Those old ways of doing things that used to get you into trouble with
each other decrease as you develop healthier patterns. Dad doesn't try
to talk on the phone and respond to his daughter's question at the
same time. Rather, he may ask the person on the phone to wait a
moment and try to address his daughter's concern or ask her to wait a
few minutes until he's off the phone. A child becomes more willing to

take a break from a game or set aside a project to respond to Dad or Mom. These small things are ways that both the parent and the child can affirm the value of each other during the instruction process. Relationship is more important than just getting the job done.

These first two steps focus on building the relationship so that it can sustain the weight of the instruction process. Simple things like eye contact, being physically close, and considering timing can do a lot to foster an attitude of cooperation. Stepparents in particular often struggle with giving instructions. Resistance seems inevitable. If you are a stepparent, concentrate on building a stronger relationship with each person in your blended family. In this way you will help children learn how to accept instruction and respond more positively in the process.

An interesting thing happens as parents incorporate these first two steps into their instruction routine. Instead of experiencing stress on the relationship whenever you give instructions, you actually see closeness develop. Parents and children are working hard to foster an attitude of cooperation, and the resulting relationship is strengthened.

STEP 3: GIVE THE INSTRUCTION →
THE CHILD ANSWERS

If you're experiencing resistance from your child, you may find that using different words in the instruction process will bring a more positive response. Proverbs 15:1 says, "A gentle answer turns away wrath, but a harsh word stirs up anger." That means that you, as a parent, should look for ways to communicate that will encourage a positive response. We recommend that you make a statement about your goal or objective before you give the instruction. "Emily, I'm trying to get things cleaned up before Dad gets home. Would you please pick up your books, shoes, and backpack in the living room?" The statement before the instruction gives children a little more information and can help them feel they're part of a team.

With young children, you may want to use the words, "You need to…now," in order to help them see that this instruction is not a suggestion and that you expect obedience. "Brian, it's time to go. You need to get into the car now" communicates that this instruction is nonnegotiable.

The older the child, the more an explanation is helpful, and not just for the purpose of showing value to the child. Older children are developing their own convictions and need to understand the reasons and guidelines behind rules and instructions. Andrew is seventeen now. He told us, "I appreciate the way my mom and dad have treated me these last few years. They don't just order me around like a little kid, but they explain why they're asking me to do something. They allow me to disagree with them at times, and I know I can discuss things with them whenever I want. Sometimes they ask me to submit even though we don't agree. The fact that they listen to me and talk about their convictions makes submitting easier to accept. I may do things differently when I'm a parent, but one thing I've decided is that I'm going to talk about instructions instead of demanding. When I'm at some of my friends' homes, I can't believe the way their parents

Asking your child to respond to instruction will reveal:
1.   that your child heard the instruction.
2.   that your child intends to do what you asked.
3.   what kind of attitude your child has.

treat them. It makes me grateful that my parents love me and show it even when they're asking me to do something."

No matter how old your child is, after you give an instruction, the child's job is to respond with a gracious answer. This reinforces the sense of relationship in the instruction process. We encourage parents to teach even young children to respond with "Okay Mom" or "Okay Dad." An answer reveals three things. First, it shows that the child has heard what you said. How many times have you gone back to check up on an assignment only to hear the child say, "But I didn't hear you"? Some parents even teach their children to repeat the instruction back by having them say, "I will…" and fill in the blank. This helps clarify the instruction for both parent and child.

The second benefit of an answer is that it teaches the child to communicate an intent to follow through. One dad said, "I like it when my son says, 'Okay Dad,' because it shows me that he's going to do what I asked."

The third benefit of a response is that you can hear what kind of attitude your child has. If it's one of those "Okaaay Mommm!" responses, you know that your child has an attitude problem. The response reveals some important things about a child's heart. Silence can mean too many things. A child may comply while harboring anger, rebellion, resentment, or defiance. Teaching children to answer after an instruction gives you a window into their hearts to see if they're responding well to the instruction. If not, a parent has the opportunity to help make some adjustments.

Some children develop patterns of arguing or making excuses when you ask them to do something. If your daughter tends to debate instructions, the underlying problem may be that she doesn't want you to tell her what to do or doesn't want to stop what she's doing to do something different. Another child may resist because he dislikes the task or shies away from anything that looks like work. Children sometimes view instructions as an intrusion into their lives. If they like the instruction, they'll follow through. If they don't, they resist.

If a child begins to argue, complain, badger, whine, or grumble when you give an instruction, stop the process. Don't continue to talk about the task. Instead talk about the way you're relating. Give a consequence if necessary, but don't allow poor relating patterns to go unchecked. It might be necessary to get out the door or leave the store first, but don't just let the problem of arguing go. Take time later to talk about any negative patterns that your child is developing.

Sometimes kids respond to an instruction by arguing because they believe they have a better idea. Parents can get caught up in these debates, believing that having these "discussions" is an honoring way to respond. After all, our children can have valid points. Discussing alternatives can occasionally be helpful, but parents who encourage it too often end up with kids who can't follow the simplest instruction without a dialogue. These children grow up to make poor employees and weak team members.

One dad set up a plan for his ten-year-old daughter, Marissa, because she always had an excuse for not following the instruction right away. "I began to feel like I was on a debate team in every conversation we had." He sat down with her one evening to talk about it. "Marissa, you have a number of great qualities that will make you successful as a wife and an employee someday, but I've noticed a problem in our interaction that I believe will hinder your success as you get older. It seems that whenever I give you an instruction, you have an excuse for not doing it right away. So I'd like us to do something different. For a while, when I give you an instruction, we're not going to discuss it. I'm going to ask you to obey right away, even though it may not be convenient. You might be in the middle of a computer game, almost ready to get to the next level, but I still want you to stop immediately and respond properly to me. When I ask you to help set the table or bring something in from the car, I want you to do it right away. Let's try this for a week and see if your response improves."

Although this dad reported resistance, he hung in there with his daughter and saw her habits change in just a few days. He was impressed with her responsiveness and even felt like he could back off from the intensity a little, which allowed his daughter the freedom to dialogue occasionally about an instruction. He didn't mind that, but if he felt they were moving back into negative patterns, he would tighten up the process again. It wasn't until Marissa was thirteen years old that she could consistently follow directions without arguing. Like Marissa, many children benefit from the structure of a routine to help them respond appropriately to instructions.

STEP 4: WAIT → THE CHILD DOES THE JOB

Some children can't seem to do anything without getting distracted. One mom, Heather, said, "When I tell my five-year-old son, James, to go get his shoes on because we've got to leave, he doesn't come back. When I go look, I find him sitting on the floor playing with his cars. And it's not just his shoes. Whenever I tell him to do something he gets sidetracked. I have to yell at him continually to get anything done."

Heather needs to use her frustration to look at the cause of the problem. James is easily distracted, but the deeper issue has to do with irresponsibility. Yes, he is only five years old, but James needs to learn to follow through with a job his mom gives him. This is the beginning of responsibility training.

Most children don't naturally feel an internal weight of responsibility. You can help develop it by watching your kids accomplish assignments and waiting for them to report back. Heather may say,

"James, we've got to go, so please get your shoes and bring them back to me. I'm going to wait right here in the doorway for you to report back." As you wait, watch for distraction. At first James may need very close monitoring, but as he realizes that he needs to report back and that Mom hasn't forgotten about the job, he will feel the pressure to accomplish the task. Children who need constant reminders lack the character quality of responsibility. They need closer supervision, smaller tasks, and more frequent times of checking in.

When children don't do what you ask them to do, yelling isn't necessary—more accountability is. It takes more work to wait or watch, but your investment now will give your children a valuable gift. One mom of a six-year-old and a three-year-old said it this way: "I defined responsibility for both my kids. We say responsibility is the ability to complete a task when no one is watching. Even my three-year-old wants to be responsible and is growing in this area."

Responsibility training happens in the instruction process. In Matthew 25, Jesus told a parable about three stewards who were given talents and the responsibility to invest them. Two of the stewards were faithful; one was not. God wants us to be faithful stewards. The roots of faithfulness are taught to children as you ask them to follow directions and report back.

STEP 5: THE CHILD CHECKS BACK →
YOU INSPECT AND RELEASE

It's been said, "Children know what you expect by what you inspect." After children report back and parents inspect what they've accomplished, everyone experiences a sense of completion. Checking back and inspecting provide opportunities for you to praise your child for obeying, teach about responsibility, and foster a positive relationship.

Inspecting and releasing add finality to the assignment. Many kids do a job part way or not at all and drift into something else. They live with an unsettled sense of anxiety because there's no closure to the instruction process. By getting the work checked, a child then experiences a sense of freedom. You give your children a gift by releasing them to go play or enjoy the rest of the evening. They're done.

One teen, Amanda, said it this way: "I always feel like my mom or dad are looking for me to do something else. I'm afraid to come out of my bedroom because they're going to give me another job."

When we talked with Amanda's parents, they said, "She never finishes things. She leaves the bathroom a mess, her room isn't clean, she doesn't do her homework, and she often doesn't practice her flute."

The relationships in this family improved when Amanda and her parents agreed on a list of expectations for Amanda and checked them off each day. Dad and Mom felt like things were getting done, and Amanda felt a sense of freedom.

Inspection takes extra energy for you as a parent, but it's an important part of the whole routine. The release you give your child is like the one in Jesus' parable. The landowner said, "Well done, good and faithful servant!" That statement, or something like it, is what your child needs to hear regularly. It brings a sense of satisfaction for a job well done. It's the reward that comes from obedience. Responsibility and faithfulness are qualities necessary for healthy relationships. This is true in our relationship with God as well. We want our kids to learn

---

A Definition of Obedience
for Young Children to Memorize

Obedience means doing what someone says, right away, without being reminded.

that one of the benefits of obeying God is that we please him. One day we'd all like to hear that statement of affirmation from God, "Well done, good and faithful servant." Children need to learn that this is God's response to them when they are responsible and obedient.

WHAT IF IT DOESN'T WORK?

The Bible gives children a job description. Ephesians 6:1 says, "Children, obey your parents in the Lord, for this is right." Children need to learn obedience because hidden within this character quality are the principles that kids need to be successful as they get older. Parents have the job of teaching obedience. We suggested five steps in a good instruction process. Each step teaches an important quality and requires action from the parent and the child:

1. Get Close Together → The Child Comes When Called
2. Consider the Timing → The Child Responds
3. Give the Instruction → The Child Answers
4. Wait → The Child Does the Job
5. The Child Checks Back → You Inspect and Release

If you're frustrated with the instruction process, identify which step is getting you off track. Practice that one part over and over again and make sure your child knows what you expect. Use consequences and refuse to continue to live the same way. By breaking down the instruction process and identifying areas that need attention and work, you will see improvement, cooperation will grow, and your relationships with your children will be closer.

Sit down with your child and explain this new routine and talk about how things will be different. Practice often to develop positive habits. Explain to your children how this routine will help them in their relationship with the Lord. When things go wrong, correct or discipline and come right back to the place where you got off track.

If five-year-old Kent, for example, doesn't come when called, go get him, but don't just go on to give the instruction. Instead, take a moment to practice calling him and having him come. Then continue on to give the instruction. If Christopher, age thirteen, grumbles when you ask him to take out the garbage, address the process: "Christopher, that's a poor response to instruction. Just leave the trash there and go sit in the hall and think about it. When you're ready we'll try again."

Even a good routine for giving instructions won't guarantee that your kids will always respond properly. But taking time to teach children to follow instructions gives them important skills they'll need to be successful in life. This instruction routine helps kids know how to respond and teaches them what to expect. Getting close teaches children that they are loved and valued. Timing helps children be responsive and willing to adjust for what's coming next. Getting an answer back helps you see indications of cooperation. Waiting while they do the task helps create the weight of responsibility, and inspecting and releasing bring closure.

When children have a hard time following instructions, it's often an indication of a deeper problem of *selfishness:* that desire to do what they want to do and how they want to do it. In the instruction routine, both the parent and the child must develop healthy patterns. In the past you may have focused on getting the job done—that's obedience. Now, you're interested in more than that. You're also concerned about valuing your child in the midst of the instruction process—that's honor. Both obedience and honor are important in relationships. Your goal is to have your kids not only help around the house but also follow instructions on the job and be better team players as they get older. And most important of all, in the process, your kids will learn to follow God's instructions and the leading of the Holy Spirit.

PUTTING IT ALL TOGETHER

When You See…

Children doing a job only part way, arguing, whining, badgering, or not following instructions, don't just focus on the task and respond with anger. Resistance is an indication of a deeper problem that needs attention.

Move into a Routine…

1. Get Close Together → The Child Comes When Called
2. Consider the Timing → The Child Responds
3. Give the Instruction → The Child Answers
4. Wait → The Child Does the Job
5. The Child Checks Back → You Inspect and Release

Because…

Teaching children how to follow instructions helps them learn responsibility, cooperation, and teamwork. They learn how to work with others and, most importantly, how to receive and obey instructions from God.

QUESTIONS FOR FURTHER DISCUSSION

1. When children learn obedience and how to follow directions, they pick up a number of skills and qualities that will help them later on in life. List several of these benefits.
2. What kinds of resistance do you get from your children when you give instructions? Why do parents sometimes give up in this area?
3. Identify one habit, good or bad, in your child that has become a routine for you in this area of giving instructions.

DIGGING DEEPER

1. Read Proverbs 1:8-9. In what way are the two analogies descriptive of the benefit of listening to instructions?
2. Saul tried to justify his disobedience by worshiping God. What was God's response in 1 Samuel 15:22? What does this tell us about the value of following God's instructions?
3. Why do you think Romans 1:29-31 and 2 Timothy 3:2-4 list disobedience to parents in lists of terrible sins?
4. This chapter makes the following statement: "When children can't see how instruction is related to relationship, they are more likely to justify unkind words or dishonoring actions when they don't like what you've told them to do. They don't understand that obedience is a demonstration of love." How does John 14:23-24 complement this idea?

BRINGING IT HOME

Have a "Follow the Clues" Treasure Hunt. In advance, place clues around the house, with each clue sending a child to the next clue, eventually ending up with a surprise at the end. Make this a cooperative effort by encouraging older children to help younger ones. You might use clues like "Look in the pocket of Dad's coat in the closet" or "The next clue is taped on the side of Sarah's favorite cereal." At the end, talk about how following instructions results in a reward. Read Proverbs 1:8-9 and talk about the benefit of listening to instructions in life.

4

He who ignores discipline comes to poverty and shame,
but whoever heeds correction is honored.

PROVERBS 13:18

"They Keep Doing the Wrong Thing"

Correction:
Giving the Gift of Wisdom

Dear Scott and Joanne,

I hate to yell at my kids. So why do I keep doing it? I'm sure it comes at least partly from my own childhood. I don't remember a lot about how my mom disciplined me, but the yelling I will never forget. It wasn't so much what she said, but the intensity in how she said it.

As a Christian now, I feel like a pioneer in my parenting. I'm discovering new and effective ways to help my kids make significant changes. I especially like your ideas about taking a Break and the Positive Conclusion. Both of these tools have helped my family, but some days are still "yelling days." More and more are not. I often find myself on my knees in my kids' room after they've fallen asleep on a "yelling day." Not only *do* I ask forgiveness from God for mistreating the beautiful gifts he has given to me, but I also pray that my kids will forget my harshness.

I know that it's only by God's grace that I'm a parent and I have to rely on that grace every day.

—Mary from Tampa, Florida

Correcting children can be exasperating. It seems that some children may be genetically predisposed to be helpful or cooperative—but most kids only pick up a broom when they want to use it to hit their brother. One mom said, "I was trying to have a garage sale last Saturday morning, but I had to spend most of my time disciplining my daughter. By noon I wanted to put her up for sale!" A dad said, "My fourteen-year-old son is so smart. It's amazing how fast he can learn to play a complicated computer game. Why can't he figure out how to work the washing machine?"

Disciplining children does take work, but it doesn't have to drain you of every last watt of energy. I (Scott) was teaching a small group of ten- and eleven-year-old boys recently. I read Proverbs 12:1: "Whoever loves discipline loves knowledge, but he who hates correction is stupid." Then our conversation went something like this:

I started, "Does it say that the person corrected is stupid?"

"No."

"What does it say?"

"The one who hates correction is stupid."

"Why do you think the Bible says that?"

"Because if you're doing the wrong thing and hate to be corrected, you keep doing the wrong thing and look stupid."

That was a good observation. I followed up with what I thought might be a helpful analogy. "Parents are like coaches. They help you see things you're not doing well so you can make changes."

Of course that raised some eyebrows. One of the boys pointed out, "Yeah, but my baseball coach yells at us all the time. I don't like that."

Another boy added, "My coach doesn't yell...but it's easier to be corrected by my coach than by my parents."

"Why?"

"I guess it's because parents know you so well."

Another student said, "It's easier to listen to a coach since you know that he's correcting you because he wants you to win."

"Well, parents want you to win at life," I offered.

After a moment of thoughtfulness one boy disagreed, "No, they just want you to stop being irritating, or to learn manners, or to get your chores done."

I had fun for the next few minutes trying to give these boys a vision for viewing their parents as coaches in life. "Parents want to train their children not only to be responsible adults but also to listen to the instruction and correction of God." I knew that if these boys could view their parents differently, they might respond better to discipline.

When my boys, Dave and Tim, were about ten and eight, I (Joanne) wanted to teach them the value of correction in their lives. Together we memorized several Bible verses from the book of Proverbs having to do with a positive view of correction. We even joked about the idea of correction being a gift. I suggested that they say "Thank you" to me every time I had to correct them. I didn't actually require this of them, but I wanted to communicate an attitude of teamwork in the correction process.

Heeding correction helps a person become wise. It's better to avoid a trap through correction than to fall into it and have to learn from experience. In fact, many of the valuable lessons of life are learned through correction in one form or another. Although children may not appreciate it, the correction they receive from you is a gift, and your persistence can provide them with the wisdom they need both now and for the future.

Training Children Requires a Toolbox

The word "discipline" used in the Old Testament is translated from the Hebrew word "chanak." It means "to train." Training implies guidance to a particular goal. Every day you're training your children to become healthy, responsible adults. Is it okay to get up and walk away in the middle of a meal? Is it acceptable to leave the table without helping to clean it up? Is it all right to eat without saying thank you to the one who prepared the meal? How will kids learn what's appropriate if you don't train them?

I (Scott) recently visited a bonsai exhibition. All the beautiful little trees had their own stories, and each was marked with a year that the plant's training began. Many of the trees had been in training for thirty or forty years, and one for as long as a hundred years. Training these trees takes time. Too much force will break a branch, and too little care returns the plant to the wild. The same is true with children. Firm, consistent discipline is needed to guide and direct your kids, but you are only an instrument in the hands of God himself. He loves your children and wants them to grow to be men and women who follow him. Parents need courage, humility, and persistence every day to face the work of confronting their kids. Correction is hard work, but it's important. The book of Proverbs records several benefits of correction:

> For these commands are a lamp, this teaching is a light, and the corrections of discipline are the way to life. (6:23)

> He who ignores discipline comes to poverty and shame, but whoever heeds correction is honored. (13:18)

A fool spurns his father's discipline, but whoever heeds correction shows prudence. (15:5)

He who ignores discipline despises himself, but whoever heeds correction gains understanding. (15:32)

Notice how the Bible ties correction to wisdom and understanding. They go together. As we correct our children, they gain wisdom. Proverbs 12:1 tells us that the wise person loves discipline. As our children mature, we want them to graciously accept correction and learn from it.

Kids make mistakes. Whether the errors are deliberate or accidental, children need a godly way to think in order to get back on track. If you implement the routine suggested in this chapter each time your kids need correction, you will train them to make changes now and build patterns for the future.

Correction is not just for children; it's a part of life for adults, too. We get corrected at work, in the family, at the gym, in the grocery store, or driving the car. If children can learn to have a positive response to confrontation when they're young, they will receive correction better as they get older. They will also be more humble and responsive to correction in their relationships with God.

Recently, I (Scott) had a clogged drain in my house. When Jack the plumber came out, he stuck a small hand-held snake into the drain but was unsuccessful at opening it up. He went back out to his truck and brought back a larger snake that had more power than the first, but was again unable to unclog the drain. I was a little worried, so I said, "What if this doesn't work?"

"I like to start easy, but if it doesn't work, I've always got something else that will." He went back out to the truck one more time and brought in the big one. It was on wheels and plugged into the wall. He removed part of the pipe and stuck the business end into the drain. Spewing all kinds of muck and making a lot of racket, he cleaned it out, and I've never had a problem since.

I like Jack's comment about drains because it's the same kind of approach we have with our kids. You have access to a number of tools as you begin the correction process. As I'm disciplining my children, I teach them that there is an easy way and a hard way to correction. "I like to start easy, but if it doesn't work, I've always got something else that will."

The correction process is important, and using the right tools produces the best results. Parents need a toolbox full of consequences to help children learn and grow. Much of the work of parenting is figuring out how best to respond to the problems you see in your kids. How can you help them change? What do you do when they don't? Children need to learn that discipline progresses. If they don't respond, the consequences get bigger. Here are some tools that provide a good correction routine for children.

TOOL 1: USE WORDS

When you need to correct your child, start with words. If children can respond to words, then no further consequence is necessary. After all, that's the mature way to handle conflict and mistakes. When a boss sees an employee doing something wrong, he starts with words of correction. If that doesn't work, he may bring in some other kind of consequence.

Caleb, three years old, was jumping on the couch. Dad, wanting to help his son change, called him over and said, "Caleb, we need to talk. You may not jump on the couch. Do you understand? If words work, then that's all we need. If you don't respond to my words, we'll have to go to the next step." Whether you're working with a preschooler jumping on the couch or a sixteen-year-old coming in past curfew, the principle is the same—start with words of correction.

We're not suggesting that every time there's an offense, you have a dialogue. If your son hits and you've already talked about hitting, then you can just proceed to the next step. What you're trying to do, however, is train your children to eventually receive correction through words without a further consequence. If a child is able to make the necessary changes after just a discussion, that's all that's needed.

Although your children may need more than words at first, over time you're moving them in the direction they need to go in order to listen to God. It's always best to respond to the whispers of the Holy Spirit in our hearts. But when we don't listen, he'll use other ways to get our attention.

Remind your kids that if words work that's all that is needed, but if they can't change with words, you'll have to try something else. Help them understand that the wise choice is to respond to words. As parents, we don't like to go further, but we will if we have to. Children need to see that their responsiveness or resistance determines the strength of the correction.

TOOL 2: HAVE THE CHILD TAKE A BREAK

When children don't respond to verbal correction, we suggest that parents move to the second tool: taking a Break. This technique follows a biblical model of correction and focuses on a child's heart, not just behavior. You can use a Break with children as young as two years old, and with modification, you can use it throughout the teen years. Developing this correction routine when children are young gives them a way to handle offenses as they get older as well.

Taking a Break looks like this. When your daughter is arguing, acting wild, demonstrating defiance, or starting to get angry, tell her

that she needs to take a Break. (You'll have to explain ahead of time
what that means.) The specific place will vary depending on the situation. With young children, that place may be on the floor in front of
the refrigerator or near the bookcase, close to where you are working.
For older children it may mean sitting on the bottom step or in the
hall. The location isn't as important as the mission: settle down and
come back ready for a debriefing.

This may sound similar to what is typically called Time Out.
Whenever we think of Time Out, we remember the story of the
woman who went into the pet store to buy a parrot. The owner, knowing that the woman went to church, said, "Lady, I can't sell you this
bird. It was owned by a sailor, and it cusses up a storm."

"Well, I know how to discipline in my family, so I'll take him
home anyway." The woman took the bird home and placed the cage
on the counter, and after a few minutes, the parrot said a bad word.
"We don't talk that way in our family," the woman told him. "If you
say another bad word, I'm going to have to put you in Time Out in
the freezer for ten minutes."

A few minutes later the bird said another bad word. Without any
comment, the woman took the bird, cage and all, and put him in the
freezer. When the timer went off, the woman opened the door and took
the cage out and placed it on the counter. "Did you learn your lesson?"

"Y-Y-Yes, L-L-Lady. But could I ask you a question? That turkey
looks like he's been in Time Out a long time. What did he do?"

Taking a Break does have one similarity to Time Out—the child
goes to a specific place to sit for a while. But the similarities end there.
In fact, we don't believe that Time Out is a constructive discipline
technique for most children. It's more like a punishment, forcing the
child to serve a sentence for an offense with the parent acting as a
policeman to keep the child in place.

In Time Out, children sit until they serve their sentence and the timer dings, but when taking a Break, your child helps determine the length of time spent there. If your son is taking a Break, he needs to stay there until he settles down. Then he should come back and talk to you. This is important for a number of reasons. If your child is ready after a minute and you have required that he stay in the Break for a longer time, you may discourage him or miss a teachable moment. On the other hand, if you set the time too short, you aren't giving enough time for God to fully work. Take the focus off the clock and put it on the heart change that needs to take place. One dad said, "My son would get so upset that he would sometimes fall asleep while taking a Break. That was okay. When he woke up he was in a better frame of mind to debrief with me."

Your posture, as a parent, is also important. Instead of being a guard to keep your child in Time Out, you now have the opportunity to stand with open arms, longing for your child to return. It's as if you're saying, "Come on now, settle down, and let's talk about this together."

Luke 15:20 offers us a beautiful image of a father waiting for his rebellious son to come back to him. The son views home as a place of safety, and although he knows he doesn't deserve to return to the same benefits, he realizes that he can come back and that Dad will accept him. The dad not only welcomes him home but reinstates all the benefits of being a son. That same picture is painted each time your child takes a Break. You can be ready and waiting for your child to return to you and enjoy family life.

A Willingness to Change

The goal of the Break is a changed heart. Although we would like to see true repentance, sorrow for doing wrong, and a desire to do what's right, those may be unrealistic in day-to-day discipline. We pray that those changes of heart will come over time. God is the one who changes a person's heart. David prayed, "Change my heart, O God," and as parents, we offer that same prayer for our children. The correction routines you use every day can prepare the way for a deeper work of the Holy Spirit in your son or daughter's life. At the least, though, a change of heart means that children must settle down and be prepared to work through the Positive Conclusion (Tool 4). If they are not ready, they must go back to the Break until they are.

For some children, in some situations, this takes two minutes or less. They just need a reminder and are ready to change. At other times, the Break may last thirty minutes or two hours. The length of time spent taking a Break is not as important as the goal—settling down and developing a willingness to change.

Heart Motivation

One of the motivations a child has to change is her desire to rejoin family life. For instance, the four-year-old who is pushing other children on the play equipment at the park may have to take a Break. She wants to change because she knows that she's missing out on playing with her friends. The eight-year-old who is having a tantrum may need to take a Break, knowing that he can't play on the computer or watch the video until he settles down.

First Corinthians 5; 2 Corinthians 2; and Matthew 18 all give instructions for handling rebellious adult children in God's family. They must miss the benefits of family life until they repent. Repentance is simply a change of heart. When others repent, we welcome them back into the inner circle of family life. There are a number of differences between disciplining an adult in God's family and disciplining a child in yours, but the motivation to change is the same.

A Versatile Tool

When children are young, taking a Break means going to a specific place to settle down. Teenagers, too, may need a cooling off period, but the Break may just come in the course of daily life. Teens need to learn that they can't hurt someone one minute and then expect a privilege the next. A teen may ask for money five minutes after speaking harshly to his mom. Rather than go on as if nothing happened, that mom may say, "I feel uncomfortable about the way you treated me a few minutes ago. I think we need to resolve that first before we can talk about money." In this way, Mom is teaching her son a very important principle about life. You can't expect to receive the benefits of family life unless you are also willing to abide by the principles that make it work. The Break for a teen may still mean sitting in the hall or going to the bedroom, but more importantly the parent is saying that life as usual must stop until we work this out.

Once your child has learned to take a Break without a tantrum or a battle, this technique can be used in the grocery store, a restaurant, or other public places. One mom told us, "I use this in the car. I tell my son that he must sit on his hands and close his mouth until he's changed his heart and settled down. We then talk about the problem and his poor response before he can interact with anyone else."

Over time, children learn how to change their hearts. This becomes a significant tool they will use for the rest of their lives. Sometimes taking a Break and the discussion that follows are all that's needed, but other times the child may still need an additional consequence. The goal is to help children change their hearts. Spending a few quiet minutes before returning to the parent can help them do that.

TOOL 3: GIVE A CONSEQUENCE

Remember Jack the plumber? We sometimes need to remind our kids, "If this doesn't work, I have something else that does." But some parents are too quick to move to Tool 3. They want to pull out the biggest tool for change, believing that the bigger the consequence, the faster the change. These parents miss out on the benefits of the first two tools. Due to your child's immaturity, you may need to use many consequences, but always keep the bigger picture in mind. You want to help your children respond to just words and accept correction well. You want them to develop wisdom. Often many small corrections are more effective than one large consequence.

Mature people will feel an internal pain when they discover that they've made a mistake or done the wrong thing. This is normal and healthy. Your child may not experience that same inner sense yet. Consequences create a kind of pain for children. This pain can motivate right behavior and true repentance.

Aaron, the father of twelve-year-old Natalie, tells about when he went to his daughter's room to confront her about the way she had yelled at him earlier:

"Natalie, I'm still feeling bad about the way you treated me in the kitchen."

"I don't have a problem," she responded flippantly.

"Well, I still feel bad about what happened."

"That's your problem. I'm fine."

"Natalie, it's important to understand something about relationships. When someone has a problem with you, then you have a problem. Relationships always have two sides, and when one person is frustrated, the other can't pretend nothing is wrong."

"You're the one with the problem. I don't have a problem, and I don't want to talk about it."

"Natalie, you do have a problem because I'm feeling hurt about the way you're talking to me. I wish that words would work and that we could just talk about this together. But you aren't willing to talk about it, and you started making phone calls when you were supposed to be taking a Break, so I'm going to have to add a consequence. I don't want to do this, but I have to try to make your life

Tips for Planning Consequences

- The younger the child, the more immediate the consequence needs to be: "Because you keep running away,
  now you have to ride in the stroller."
- As children get older, tie consequences logically to life:
  "Because you're not finishing your homework assignments, you'll have to get them checked each day by
  me." (Lack of responsibility requires greater accountability.) "Rachel, since you didn't listen to my warning
  and continued to be wild and broke the lamp, I'm
  going to ask you to earn the money to replace
  it."(When children are unresponsive to words of correction, they need to experience the negative consequences of their actions.)
- You might ask yourself, "What privilege is my child
  misusing?" to help determine the consequence. Tie
  privileges and responsibility together: "Since you are
  not sticking to the time limits we agreed upon, now
  you lose the privilege of playing on the computer for
  a while." "Jim, because you weren't responsible with
  your bike and left it on the front lawn overnight,
  you're going to lose the privilege of riding it today."
- Choose constructive consequences: "Because you
  continue to be mean to your brother, I want you
  to choose three ways to show kindness to him."
- Teach through natural consequences: "I'm sorry that
  you got scratched. That sometimes happens when you
  play rough with the cat."

more uncomfortable with outside pain so that you will be motivated to deal with the problem between us. My goal is for you to eventually have an internal pain that doesn't require consequences, but until then, I'm going to have to use consequences to motivate you to make changes."

Aaron remained calm and continued, "First of all, you won't be able to be with your friends until we deal with this problem. I'm also going to start by taking your stereo out of your room. You will lose the privilege of having a stereo." He proceeded to remove the stereo and place it in the hall. Natalie didn't seem to care. Aaron said, "I want you to think about this for fifteen minutes. If you aren't willing to change, then I'm going to take the door off your bedroom."

Awhile later Aaron returned. Natalie still didn't respond, so Aaron proceeded to take her door off its hinges and place it in the hall. "That's all the consequence I'm going to give you for now. I'll expect that the next thing to happen is that we'll talk about this problem." Aaron left Natalie to think about it. About an hour later, she came out to talk. The discussion about the way they relate together was helpful, and Natalie ended up apologizing. Because Aaron felt like Natalie was genuinely repentant, he returned her stereo and door to her room and thanked her for working the problem through to a conclusion.

This kind of discipline doesn't view consequences as a sentence for doing wrong or a way to balance the scales of justice. Rather, it sees consequences as tools for helping children change. God does the same thing with us. Often he will allow us to bump into problems and circumstances in our lives to motivate us to adjust or make the right choices. Parents shouldn't regard consequences as paybacks for wrongdoing, but should instead look at them as ways to motivate a change of heart.

A wise parent uses a variety of consequences. Some work more effectively on one child than another, and even the same child will

respond well one time and need something different the next. Productive consequences often require planning. If a child is not responding to your words or to a Break, it's important to have the next step
thought out and ready to go. Spur-of-the-moment consequences spoken out of anger rarely bring about the change you're looking for.
Instead of trying to think quickly in the heat of anger, maybe you just
need to say, "Son, you need to take a Break. There will be a consequence, but I need time to settle down and think about it myself."

After you give a consequence, a child must report back for Tool 4.

TOOL 4: END WITH
A POSITIVE CONCLUSION

You need a combination of tools to do a complete job with many of
your household tasks. The same is true with correcting your children.
Tool 4, the Positive Conclusion, is a tool that's used along with one
or more of the other three. Sometimes you'll use the first tool: words.
At other times you'll have to move to bigger tools to help your child
change his heart. In any case, after he or she takes a Break or you give
a consequence, the child comes back to you for the final tool: the Positive Conclusion. This last tool helps do the cleanup work. It's a discussion about what went wrong and how to change for next time.

When correction takes place, often a sense of tension lingers
between the parent and the child. The Positive Conclusion helps you
both sort out the issues and develop a plan for next time. It enables
you and your child to feel reunited and reconciled after the correction, allowing your child to move on without feeling discouraged
or angry.

In Scripture we see the Positive Conclusion modeled as God disciplined people. With Adam and Eve, for example, the consequence
for sin was expulsion from the garden. Afterwards, though, God

made clothes for them and gave them a promise that someday the seed of the woman would conquer the serpent. God left the discipline situation on a positive, hopeful note.

Here's What It Looks Like

If you have young children, up to age eleven or twelve, we encourage you to use three questions and a statement for your Positive Conclusion. (Children as young as two or three can also learn this, depending how verbal they are.) This predictable routine helps kids know what to expect and gives them a plan for how to think about offenses in the future. Over time, they learn that the Positive Conclusion is something that comes at the end of every discipline situation. It's an important part of the correction process.

When your child returns after a Break or a consequence, your attitude is very important. Welcome your child back in a warm and accepting way, not with a harsh attitude of condemnation. If you're still struggling with your own anger over the offense, maybe you need a few minutes alone before you can work with your child in a helpful way.

To start the Positive Conclusion, ask the *first question,* "What did you do wrong?" This question helps kids take responsibility for their own part of the problem. Many children will want to blame others for their mistakes or focus on the injustice instead of their poor response to it. Parents sometimes then make the mistake of arguing with a child or defending themselves and others.

Mom heard Becky yell from the other room, "Mom, Luke hit me!"

"She took my book!" Luke returned.

As Mom enters the room, she says, "It sounds like both of you need a Break. Becky, please go to the hall, and Luke, go to the top step." Each child knows that the next thing that happens is they must return to Mom. When Becky comes back, Mom says, "Okay Becky, what did you do wrong?"

"Well, he hit me."

"I didn't ask you what Luke did wrong. We'll take care of that in a minute. What I asked is, What did you do wrong?"

"I took his book."

"All right. It looks like that contributed to the problem."

Mom continues the Positive Conclusion with Becky, and then separately with Luke when he comes to her. When she's done she sends them back to play together again.

When children learn to answer this first question, they learn humility and courage. Confession is a spiritual issue. God asks us to confess our sins as the first step toward accepting his forgiveness.

Positive Conclusions in the Bible

- Peter denied Christ three times. After his resurrection, Jesus asked Peter three times, "Do you love me?" After Peter responded positively, Jesus welcomed him back into ministry to take care of his sheep (John 21:15-17).
- Israel lost the battle of Ai because Achan disobeyed. God disciplined the nation and then told them not to be afraid but to continue on with the conquest of Palestine: "Do not be discouraged.... Into your hand I will deliver the city" (Joshua 8:1,18).
- David committed adultery with Bathsheba. After the consequence of losing their child, Bathsheba got pregnant again, and God spoke through Nathan to give a name to the child. This reaffirmed God's love for David and encouraged David that his sin would not hinder God's guidance and protection (2 Samuel 12).

Children must learn to take responsibility for their part of the problem, however small it may be.

The *second question* is, "Why was that wrong?" This gives you an opportunity to teach. When Luke is called out of the playroom for hitting and you come to this question, you're able to talk about character and values, not just behavior. Luke shouldn't hit, because hitting isn't kind. Over and over again, you may pull Luke out of the playroom, and each time he's going to talk about why his behavior is wrong. You don't have to spend a huge amount of time analyzing, lecturing, or persuading. Just ask the question and let him respond.

Over time, you will not only help Luke change, but you will also teach him why he's changing. If your child can't answer this question, you have the opportunity to explain the values behind your rules. Give a brief explanation and then ask the question again and have your child respond.

The *third question* is, "What are you going to do differently next time?" Here the conversation moves in a positive direction. Kids need to be prepared to handle the temptations of life. What should Luke do instead of hitting the next time his sister takes his book? What should Becky do when she wants the book that Luke has? How should kids handle conflict, injustice, sarcasm, or meanness? This question helps both you and your child brainstorm about the "next times" of life. It becomes an excellent exercise in right thinking.

A child who is stuck in a negative pattern will, no doubt, have to go through a Positive Conclusion several times during the day. Each time she must verbalize what she did wrong, why it was wrong, and what she can do differently next time. You can't expect immediate change, but be patient and continue on. Even when children know the right thing to do, it's hard to change. So continue using the Positive Conclusion even when your child is just verbalizing the right answer but is unable to do it. Change takes time. In essence, you can do therapy with your kids, helping them think and act in more God-honoring ways.

After the three questions it's important to make *a final positive statement* that goes something like this: "Okay, go try again." That statement communicates affirmation to your child, saying, "I believe in you. You can do the right thing. You may have made a mistake, but now you know what to do. Go for it." It reminds us of the woman caught in adultery in John 8. After it was all over Jesus said, "Go now and leave your life of sin." This affirmation freed her from continual self-condemnation and gave her a clean slate to go and try again. Your children need that.

You may say, "My kids aren't going to answer these questions," and maybe you're right. They won't answer them unless you teach them how to go through this process. These questions are an important part of a helpful correction routine. So take some time and teach your children how to answer these questions for themselves and for you. If they aren't cooperative, maybe they need to continue their Break until they're ready to respond.

Closure for Older Children

When children are older, you may not want to use the three questions and a statement, but conflict or discipline always needs closure. The teenage boy who loses phone privileges for a week, or the teen girl who is sent to her room for her angry outburst, both need a Positive Conclusion. Talk about the problem and how they might handle it differently next time. Children who grow up using the Positive Conclusion learn that conflict requires resolution and that talking about problems is a healthy way to bring closure.

The Positive Conclusion also helps children learn how to think rightly about mistakes. Many adults, in fact, would benefit from asking themselves these three questions and making a statement when in a difficult situation. Some people, after making a mistake, say things to themselves such as "I'll never get it right" or "I'm stupid." A Positive Conclusion helps us think rightly about offenses and go on to do things differently next time.

HOW PARENTAL ANGER CONFUSES THE PROCESS

Using words, having children take a Break, and giving consequences, followed by a Positive Conclusion, teach children a valuable routine for correction. Kids learn what's appropriate, what's not, and why. They develop healthy patterns of behavior, begin to think differently, and change their hearts. They learn how to accept correction and develop wisdom. Your harshness, however, confuses the learning process. Instead of thinking, "I'm here taking a Break because I did something wrong," the child thinks, "I'm here taking a Break because I upset Mom." The child's focus changes from correcting what he or she did wrong to avoiding your anger. It's important to remember that your anger is helpful for identifying problems but not good for solving them. When you're tempted to respond harshly, be careful to take a moment and think about what you need to teach in this situation. It's easy to react with anger when your kids do the wrong thing, but it's more helpful to move into a constructive correction routine.

Dad yells, "I've had it! I called you five times and you didn't come, so I'm not taking you to the party!" The child gets a mixed message. Is missing the party the consequence for not coming when called, or is it the consequence for making Dad angry? Children who grow up with explosive parents learn to focus more on pleasing people than on living with a conviction of right and wrong. They may learn to make changes in life, but not because they're determined to do what's right. Rather, they make changes to avoid upsetting people; they become people pleasers or just plain sneaky. As kids, they believed that what they did was okay as long as Mom or Dad didn't find out. When you make a mistake and correct in anger, it's important to come back to your child and talk about it afterwards. Clarify what was wrong, why the consequence was given, and apologize for your harshness.

WHAT IF MY CHILD JUST GOES THROUGH THE MOTIONS?

Some parents feel that a Break isn't working because they don't see their child's heart changing right away. As parents we're looking for the most efficient way to help our kids grow and mature so that life now and in the future will be smoother for them. If you examine the way you discipline, you may discover that you spend a lot of time on behavior modification—getting your children to do the right thing—but the heart is not touched.

Parents who are content to focus on behavior may be teaching their kids image management: the ability to appear good, clean, and nice. But God is concerned with the heart and its importance to our lives. The problem is we have only limited influence on how fast a child's heart changes. You could force behavior change and move on, but sometimes your child is still angry, rebellious, or resistant. The better choice is to take time to help your child do the deeper heart work necessary for lasting change to take place. That is where a Break can be so helpful. Your child needs to stay in the Break until ready to go through a Positive Conclusion and talk about what he or she did wrong and why it was wrong. The Break and Positive Conclusion help children address their hearts, not just their behavior. Heart changes may take longer than behavior change, but the end result will be deeper and more significant.

The market is full of behavior modification techniques today. In one week, two new families came to us for counseling. They were both using the same program that was wildly popular at the time, but it wasn't working. The strategy looks like this: When a child argues, you say, "That's one." If the child continues, you say, "That's two," and if the child still continues, you say, "That's three, take five." The child must now take a five-minute Time Out before rejoining family life. If you're interested in just changing behavior, this approach might work, but it lacks the depth needed to address the heart. This approach also doesn't teach children an adult way of relating to life. After all, when you make a mistake at work, how many times does the boss turn to you and say, "That's one"? It's just not the best way to help kids make lasting changes.

Behavior modification is not enough because it doesn't address the deeper issues of the heart. The correction routine outlined in this chapter helps children make lasting changes. It can be used with simple problems as well as with more ingrained challenges in a child's life such as defiance, impulsiveness, meanness, and emotional explosiveness.

Five-year-old Brittany has a problem managing her emotions. She blows up at the smallest irritation. One day when her mom saw Brittany getting frustrated, she tried to head off the explosion early. First, Mom tried to talk about it by just pointing out what she saw. "Brittany, you are snapping at me. Could you please be more honoring in the way you talk to me?" Brittany wasn't able to change with just words, so Mom moved to Tool 2. She sent Brittany to take a Break in the hall. Brittany yelled and stomped all the way there. After a while she came back, and Mom led Brittany through the Positive Conclusion.

"What did you do wrong?"

"I got angry."

"Well, it's not wrong to be angry, but first you snapped at me, and then you yelled and stomped and said some mean things on the way to the Break. Do you understand that those things are wrong?"

"Yes."

"Good, then I'm going to ask you the question again. What did you do wrong?"

"I yelled, stomped, and said mean things."

"Okay. Why is that wrong?"

"I don't know."

"It's wrong because it's not kind. It's hurtful to me and to others. It's just not the right way to treat other people, even when you're not happy with them. Do you understand that?"

"Yes."

"Then I'm going to ask that question again. Why was that wrong?"

"It wasn't kind."

"Okay, what are you going to do differently next time?"

"I'm not going to yell."

"That's good. Next time that I say no when you ask for something,

---

Notice the emphasis on the heart instead of behavior in the following verses:

- Trust in the LORD with all your heart. (Proverbs 3:5)
- Guard your heart, for it is the wellspring of life. (Proverbs 4:23)
- The heart is deceitful above all things and beyond cure. Who can understand it? (Jeremiah 17:9)
- Man looks at the outward appearance, but the LORD looks at the heart. (1 Samuel 16:7)

I'd like you to either be quiet or respond by saying okay. Do you think you can do that?"

"Yes."

"Good. Now, because you had such a difficult time going to the Break, I'm going to send you again right now. I want to see you do that without stomping or treating me unkindly. Do you understand?"

"I'm fine now. I don't want to take a Break."

"I know you don't want to, but I'm sending you to take a Break because of the way that you responded earlier. You don't have to stay there long, but when you come back we're going to talk about it. I want to see if you can respond properly to correction."

This time Brittany returned to the hall quietly. Then she quickly came back. Mom again said, "Okay Brittany, what did you do wrong?"

"I stomped off when you sent me to a Break."

"Why was that wrong?"

"It's not treating you kindly."

"You're right. What are you going to do differently next time?"

"I'll say okay."

"That's good. In fact, it's great. If you'll do that you'll be very successful when people correct you. Okay, go ahead and we'll try again later."

Brittany's mom used a Break and a Positive Conclusion to help Brittany begin to make some significant changes. The plan wasn't a "one-time correction and everything will be fine" kind of approach. Significant change rarely comes in one session. The continual work of going over the same issues several times a day, admitting that she was wrong, and restating the right thing to do will help Brittany make heart-level changes as she grows.

Whether your children have habitual problems that need adjustment or they're actually being defiant, the four tools in this chapter give you a correction routine that will work. Remember, kids learn best from repetition and consistency over time. Using the same routine for correction each time your children need redirection will help them make the heart-level changes necessary and provide the character they need to be responsive to God's correction. This process works because it follows a biblical model of change. Confessing, taking responsibility, being humble, choosing a better course of action, and committing to do what's right are all part of godliness. Ending on a positive note empowers children to change. It may not happen overnight, but the continual, daily work of parenting will help develop the wisdom in your children that can only come from healthy correction.

PUTTING IT ALL TOGETHER

When You See...
Misbehavior, defiance, wildness, continual mistakes, and childhood foolishness, take the time to correct.

Move into a Routine...
Start with words and talk about what you see and what needs to change. Give children specific things you want them to do, not just condemnation for a wrong action. If words don't work, use a Break to help children change their hearts, not just behavior. If a Break isn't working, add a consequence. Remember, change takes place over time, and your patience and persistence can do a lot to help your children make the necessary adjustments in behavior and learn the valuable character qualities they'll need. Always end the correction with a Positive Conclusion, helping the child talk through and learn from the experience.

Because…

Correction is a part of life. Children need to receive correction willingly because it helps them become wise and effective. A good response to correction is important in education, employment, and spiritual life. Your present correction routine will teach children how to respond to God's correction as they grow and mature in their relationship with him.

QUESTIONS FOR FURTHER DISCUSSION

1. What is a habit you're trying to change in yourself? Change isn't easy. How can you be firm with your children and at the same time be empathetic about the challenge of change?
2. Compare and contrast a "policeman" approach to parenting and a "coach" approach. How are they different? What kinds of things can you do or say as a parent to demonstrate a coaching attitude with your kids?
3. List several ways that the Positive Conclusion contributes to a godly way of thinking about mistakes.

DIGGING DEEPER

1. Read Proverbs 13:18. Why do you think heeding correction results in honor?
2. Read Galatians 6:1. What things are mentioned in this verse about a godly way of correcting? How can you apply these to parenting?
3. Read 2 Timothy 4:2. Paul is giving Timothy instructions about correcting people under Timothy's care. What words are used that describe the way that he was to correct and how might that apply to correcting children?

4. How does God correct people today? How can your
    approach to correction prepare your children to receive
    correction from God?

BRINGING IT HOME

Imagine that you and your children have to create an operating man-
ual for a family. Make sure the children know this is hypothetical by
saying something like, "If you had to create a family, how might it
operate?" List several offenses and consequences that might be used to
keep children and parents moving in the right direction. You might
ask questions like, "What should happen to a child who has a bad
attitude?" "What if someone is mean to his brother?" "What should
be done about messy rooms?" "How should chores be handled?"
"What should happen if parents start ranting and raving?" Discuss the
ramifications of each of the suggestions. Talk about the benefits of
correction and the consequences of a lack of correction in family life.

5

Do everything without complaining or arguing.
PHILIPPIANS 2:14

"They Won't Accept No for an Answer"

Accepting Limits:
Giving the Gift of Contentment

Dear Scott and Joanne,

Today my five-year-old daughter heard the ice cream truck and demanded that I buy her some ice cream. I told her no because it gets expensive to buy it from the ice cream man every day. I suggested that we have some ice cream out of our freezer a little later. I went to the bathroom, and she continued to badger me through the door and even pounded on it. I told her to leave me alone in the bathroom unless it was an emergency. She wouldn't stop. When I came out I was pretty upset.

I know that I should have disciplined her earlier, but I didn't. I started getting both of us a bowl of ice cream, hoping to keep her quiet so she wouldn't wake up the baby. Anyway, to make a long story short, I lost it and broke a plate in the sink. Needless to say, she didn't get any ice cream.

After thinking about it, I realize that I need to move into a discipline mode more quickly when she gets demanding and won't accept no for an answer. I can see that if I don't help my daughter deal with this now she'll grow up to be an unhappy, demanding person.

Thanks for all your help.

—Jenn from Princeton, New Jersey

You may have heard parents say, "If I had a quarter for every time my children ask me for something, I'd be a millionaire." It's true that kids come to Mom and Dad countless times to ask for things. "Can I have a snack?" "Will you take me to the store?" "May I watch a video?" "Will you play with me?" And the list goes on and on. Parents often say yes and enjoy doing so because they love to please their children, to see them happy, and to enjoy their friendship. But sometimes things don't work out, and we as parents have to say no to a request. That doesn't mean we don't love our children. It just means that we know more than they do, or must balance other priorities, and a no answer seems best for everyone at that time.

Some children have a hard time seeing the bigger picture and can only focus on their own disappointment. These kids may become demanding and refuse to accept limits. They end up sacrificing relationships to get what they want. The sad thing is that demanding children often learn they can accomplish their goals, but in doing so, they hurt others. They give in to the ultimate expression of selfishness—taking from others without considering others' needs or desires.

We like the definition a mom we know uses for demandingness: "Expecting the world to stop and change just for me." Demanding kids moan and groan or engage in other negative relating habits when they're disappointed. Arguing, badgering, and whining are just three common responses, and children do them without thinking. Parents are easily drawn into the conflict, and everyone ends up feeling frustrated.

LEARNING TO BE CONTENT

When children can't accept no as an answer, they're dealing with a deeper spiritual issue: an inability to handle disappointment. Because of our sinful nature, at times we all develop a "me first" attitude. We want life to be our way, and we want it now! Some parents make the mistake of confusing demandingness with persistence, thinking that their children have a good quality of determination. The difference is that *persistence* pursues a goal in spite of obstacles. *Demandingness* risks relationships to obtain that goal. Persistence isn't wrong, but sacrificing relationship with others for one's own agenda is. Treating others unkindly when you don't get your way says that you value what you want more than you value the people around you. It's at that point that desire becomes sin.

One dad said it this way: "I taught my twelve-year-old son the difference between a demand, a desire, and a wish. When he comes down to dinner and sees spaghetti, he might express a wish saying, 'I wish there were meatballs in this sauce.' Or he might come down and say, 'I want meatballs in my spaghetti sauce.' That's a 'desire' response, stronger than a wish. But when he comes down and says, 'I'm not eating that spaghetti without meatballs,' and makes unkind statements to his mother, he's moved to demandingness. This distinction has helped my son because now he tries to move demands back to desires or wishes."

One of the signs of spiritual maturity is that a person exchanges demandingness for contentment. Paul said in Philippians 4:11 that contentment didn't automatically appear but it was something he learned: "I have learned to be content whatever the circumstances." Contentment is being satisfied and grateful for what you have instead of grumbling about what you don't have. It is a spiritual quality that adds peace and joy to our lives without the feeling that we need something more.

As with many spiritual conditions, contentment is learned at home. Children are often tempted to be demanding with parents and others. When we, as parents, teach our children to accept a no answer graciously, we are moving them toward contentment. This doesn't mean that your children need to release any sense of ambition in life. It does mean that as they work toward a goal, they maintain an internal peace and the ability to accept limitations and value relationships in the process.

Every family develops routines to handle situations where parents give a no answer. The three-year-old bursts into tears because he can't have candy in the store. The ten-year-old says, "Fine!" and huffs off to the other room when her mom says no to more computer time. The fifteen-year-old starts yelling at his mom because she won't drive

---

Helpful Definitions for You and Your Kids

- **Persistence** pursues a goal in spite of obstacles.
- **Demandingness** risks relationships to obtain a goal.
- **Contentment** is being satisfied and grateful for what you have instead of grumbling about what you don't have.
- **Arguing** uses logic and emotion to change someone's mind without considering how the intensity of the discussion is hurting the relationship.

him to his friend's house. Each of these situations provides an opportunity to teach contentment. Many parents react harshly to the selfishness in their kids, however, and the battle routine begins.

As with many areas of parenting, if you want your children to change, you must make some adjustments first. Without realizing it, parents sometimes develop relational routines that encourage demandingness in their children. Before you can adjust the routine, you need to discover what your existing pattern looks like. If your children respond poorly to a no answer, take a few moments to analyze their responses and your typical reaction. What is the first thing said? How can you tell this is going to be one of those times again? What are the first signals? How do you typically respond? Do you go into a defensive mode? Harshness? Justification? How does your child respond to that? You will quickly discover a pattern that has developed, like a dance where each person reacts to the other, back and forth, and back again.

After thinking about what happens when her son badgers, one mom told us, "All I do is respond to his questions. There's nothing wrong with that. In fact, I thought it was good to talk with your kids… It's just that he won't quit." It's true that talking with kids is helpful most of the time, but when parents indulge badgering children, they become part of the problem.

As a parent, you've probably discovered that even when you do good things with your kids, at times problems develop and you have to make adjustments. As you examine your current routine, you may discover that in an attempt to do something helpful such as talk things through, you've actually encouraged something unhelpful such as arguing. You may find that you're not actually doing something wrong, but the pattern that's developed has become unhealthy.

After you identify your patterns, use some of the ideas in this chapter to slow things down, respond differently, and begin developing new routines when your child asks for something. Refuse to dance the same old way, and your child will change as well. Begin to point out the tendencies and habits you see and look for constructive alternatives. You will not only see family life improve, but you'll set the stage for your children to grow in contentment. Someday your children will be able to say, like Paul in Philippians 4:12, "I know what it is to be in need, and I know what it is to have plenty. I have learned the secret of being content in any and every situation, whether well fed or hungry, whether living in plenty or in want." Children can learn contentment, in part, by knowing how to receive a no answer from a parent and accept it graciously.

DEMANDINGNESS SYMPTOM 1: ARGUING

Arguing can be defined this way: Using logic and emotion to change someone's mind without considering how the intensity of the discussion is hurting the relationship.

The child who is prone to argue will often start with "Why?" in order to find ammunition. You, of course, view it as a harmless question, and since you have the answer on the tip of your tongue, you graciously pass it on. The child responds with "But..." and now you're both off and running. These kinds of discussions aren't bad (in fact they can occasionally be helpful), but some children use them as manipulative techniques to get their own way. Arguing can become an irritating habit and drain your relationship.

Children who argue have good character qualities like persistence, perseverance, determination, creativity, and an ability to communicate ideas. The problem with arguing is that your child views you as an obstacle, a mountain to tunnel through. The child who argues often lacks sensitivity and doesn't take your feelings into account. Your challenge as a parent is to encourage the positive qualities and remove the negative ones.

Lydia, a single mom, feels like she has to be a courtroom attorney every time she says no to her son, Jackson. Here's a typical example:

"Mom, can I watch a video tonight?"

"No, not tonight."

"But why? I've got my homework done."

"You've watched a lot of TV these past few days, and I think it would be good for you to find something else to do."

"But I don't want to do anything else."

"Why don't you read a book?"

"I don't want to read a book. I've wanted to watch this show for a week. I haven't been able to because Randall had the video. Now I've got it back."

"No, not tonight."

"Why?"

And on and on it goes.

Jackson wouldn't accept no for an answer and continually looked for ways to persuade his mom to change her mind. As Lydia evaluated the interaction, she saw that they both had contributed to a negative pattern. As she began making adjustments, she saw significant change in her son as well.

Changing Your Mind

The first thing Lydia noticed was that she would make a decision but then change her mind in response to the arguing, and by doing so, actually encourage it. "It's hard because sometimes Jackson will reveal new information in the process that's very persuasive, and I find myself willing to reevaluate the situation. Unfortunately, I'm left with a predicament. I don't mind reevaluating, but he seems to have this attitude that I owe him something. I just don't like the way he's treating me in the process." Lydia learned to postpone the decision until she had all the facts. She would say things like, "Tell me more." And, "Let me think about that for a few minutes."

Changing your mind isn't always bad, but you need to make a distinction for your child between the new information and the process of how you got it: "I would like to change my mind here, but I'm feeling uncomfortable with the way you're talking to me. Your arguing is not helpful in our relationship, and I don't want to encourage it by changing my mind. You have a good point, but your exasperated tone of voice is demanding and disrespectful."

You may choose to stick to a no answer in spite of new and persuasive information. As a parent you're not just making a decision based on information, but you're also looking at how your child presents that information and what you want this child to learn. After all, character is more important than the decision.

Discussion or Argument?

Lydia also noticed that she would engage in unhealthy arguments with Jackson when the issue was secondary and winning became the priority for both of them. One of the reasons that arguing is dangerous to a relationship is that it sets the parties at odds. Most parents feel uncomfortable with arguments, but they don't know why or what to do about it. The child who wants to argue puts the parent in an awkward position. When the child takes on the role of attacker, the parent becomes the defender. This relating pattern sets the two up as opponents instead of partners.

The difference between an argument and a discussion has to do with relationship. When the issue becomes more important than the people discussing it, the discussion has turned into an argument. The best way to teach or even discuss a problem is with you and your child on the same side of the net. Instead of allowing issues to come between you, look for ways to make the issue the opponent and you and your child partners in solving it. Sometimes an argument can move into a discussion with a little adjusting on your part. "What are you hearing me say?" "Let's both try to think of advantages and disadvantages of your watching a video tonight." With these kinds of statements, you refuse to become an opponent and continue to look for areas of cooperation. The discussion will give you an opportunity to encourage the good aspects of your child's character.

Choosing the Best Response

Don't give in just because your children have good reasons. Teach them how to present those reasons graciously. A lot of people in life are right but present their case in a dishonoring way. Teach children that being right is not enough. They also have to be respectful in their presentation. Consider the next two illustrations of parents who accomplished the goal of reducing arguing in different ways.

One dad said, "I sometimes continue to say no until my daughter accepts my answer and then, after the discussion is over, determine whether to reevaluate the decision based on her response. If she gets angry and mean with me, I point out her demandingness. If she has a gracious response, I consider whether I can change my answer."

Another dad had a different approach. "As I evaluated my interaction with Joey, I discovered that I would say no too early in the dialogue. This would move him into an attacking mode because he was frustrated that I didn't hear him out. I realized that I was making a decision too quickly in the process. As I spent more time listening and affirming his ideas before I made a decision, I saw a change in his attitude toward my final answer."

Both of these parents accomplished the goal of helping their children learn to accept a no answer. The first dad determined to say no to train his daughter to respond graciously. The second dad postponed his answer to let his son feel heard. Because children and parents are all different, you must look for things that will work for your family. By evaluating your present routines and making some well-planned adjustments, you will see change in your children as well. Your work in this area will teach a valuable lesson about life. A child who is prone to argue needs to learn to be more sensitive to other people's feelings. Winning an argument doesn't really mean you win. A good salesman knows that you might win an argument and lose the client. A child needs to learn when to stop pushing.

Discussions can bring out needed information to make informed decisions, but arguing has a hurtful edge that detracts from relationships. The things that parents argue about with their children are often not even important. Paul reminded young Timothy to be careful of these kinds of arguments when he said, "Don't have anything to do with foolish and stupid arguments, because you know they produce quarrels" (2 Timothy 2:23). That sounds like good advice for family life, too.

DEMANDINGNESS SYMPTOM 2: BADGERING

A badger is a burrowing animal with an amazing amount of persistence. Badgers have extraordinary physical and emotional strength and a tenacious approach to life's challenges. Children who like to badger usually have dominating personalities and confident persistence, challenging anyone who blocks their path. Michele shared this example of her four-year-old daughter, Kayla, who had already learned the art of badgering.

Kayla: Mom, can I have a snack?

Mom: No, I'm making lunch, and it'll be ready in fifteen minutes.

Kayla: Could I have just a little snack?

Mom: No, you need to wait a few minutes. Here, you can help me if you'd like.

Kayla: Only if I can eat some of it.

Mom: No, I want you to wait just a few minutes.

Kayla: Could I have a cookie?

Mom: Kayla, what did I say? We'll eat in a few minutes.

Kayla: Could I have a drink of milk?

Mom: No.

Kayla: Can I have some apple juice?

Mom: Kayla, stop asking me for something to eat or drink.

Kayla: My bear wants something to eat. He's hungry.

And on and on it goes.

When a child resorts to badgering, the goal is to wear the parent down in order to change the no answer to a yes answer. It's amazing how many different ways a child can rephrase the same question, hoping that this time it will result in a different response. Badgering is very tiring for a parent, and that's probably why it works sometimes. You may have heard the story about one child telling another, "If you want a kitten, start by asking for a horse."

Sometimes the badgering is simply an attempt to gain attention and lots of it. Question after question after question. Some children seem to have the strategy down to a science. But parents can be just as determined. One mom tried so hard to resist her son's badgering that he finally threw his hands up in frustration and said, "Mom, you can be so stubborn."

Any parent who has a badgering child feels the unending tension in the relationship. Parents may want to hide or even look for ways to avoid their son or daughter. Some parents say they cringe when they see that child coming. These parents feel bad, but the tension in the relationship has become a real irritation.

Children who use badgering tend to be self-focused and can't see what their barrage of questions and comments is doing to relationships. Parents who experience this kind of tension may find it helpful to reflect their feelings in a gentle way, helping to develop the sensitivity that's desperately needed. "I'm feeling uncomfortable with your question because I think I already answered it." Or, "I'm not sure how to respond here. I don't want to talk about this subject anymore, but you keep bringing it up." Or, "I feel like you're running over me with a truck. Let's talk about something else before I get smashed to bits!"

Many parents encourage the badgering by giving in to it. One dad said, "My son keeps it up until he finds something I'll say yes to. He'll even change the subject and ask for something completely different. It seems as if he needs a yes answer in order to leave the conversation. I imagine that if I keep saying no, he'll eventually ask something like, 'Dad, could I take out the trash?' just so I'll say yes to him. We're stuck in a pattern. Somehow, we need to figure out how to end without my saying yes."

If you have a child who demonstrates demandingness by badgering, you first need to point it out so that your child understands the problem. You might say, "Son, we're back in the badgering routine here. I want you to stop now and not ask me for anything else for the next hour. We can continue to talk or be together, but no more permission questions for a while." When children badger and you grant permission for even good things, you may be fostering demandingness in your children. Badgering is a selfish way for children to get what they want.

DEMANDINGNESS SYMPTOM 3: WHINING

Children who whine are disappointed with life and use moaning and groaning to inform others. They use a high-pitched voice or a drawn-out monotone to mope, complain, bellyache, and grumble until everyone else around them feels irritated. It's as if they want company at their little misery party, and they'll keep advertising until everyone else joins them. This gets so irritating that many parents give in just to stop the noise. Parents know they can end the whining by solving the problem, but, inadvertently, this just encourages more whining instead of teaching children a better way.

Jackie's daughter, Tia, had a problem with whining. "It's definitely the tone of voice. That's how I know she's at it again. You can hear her voice change to that irritating whine. It reminds me of a squeaky door. I hate it. I tell her to stop, and she says, 'But Moooooommmmm,' in the same voice. It drives me nuts. I send her to her room, and she just goes there and pouts. Nothing seems to work. When Tia's not happy, no one is happy."

Children whine because it works. It either gets Mom to change her mind or gains sympathy and attention. Children who haven't learned to handle disappointment can use whining as a type of revenge to get back at the parent who says no.

Parents often get angry when the whining begins. Next time you see this pattern, determine to make a change. Instead of yelling or whining yourself, move into a more constructive routine. Recognize the situation as an opportunity to develop godly character in your child. Use that whining voice as a flag that demandingness is raising its ugly head again. As you move into a new routine, you'll find that your child will also have to make significant changes. Your child needs to learn to accept disappointment. Life provides many opportunities to demonstrate contentment, whether you're two or thirty-two. Teaching children to respond properly now will help them relate to life's challenges in a healthier way as they get older.

The Developing Contentment Curriculum

Arguing, badgering, and whining are three ways that children act out the demandingness that's in their hearts. One mom, in desperation, said, "My son does all three, and he can do them all at the same time!" Whenever you see these symptoms, you know that your child is experiencing a selfish attitude and needs the "Developing Contentment Curriculum." Once you have a plan, you won't feel the need to react in anger but can instead begin the process of teaching your child about contentment. You can now view the wrong behavior as an opportunity.

Contentment comes from trust in God. Most of the time, your theological goals may just be in the back of your mind, providing motivation for you to continue the discipline process. The older children get, however, the more you can share with them about godliness and why you are taking such a strong stand in certain areas. One dad remembered a key turning point with his teenage daughter when he approached her problem of complaining from a spiritual perspective. "Honey, I know you are just focusing on the limits I'm placing on you, but would you think about something else just for a minute. Our relationship is important to me, and I try to say yes to you whenever I can. Sometimes I have to say no, and when I do, I feel hurt because you attack me as if I'm the enemy. Your persistence hurts our relationship. That's why God talks about contentment in the Bible. Contentment is the ability to be grateful for what you already have instead of complaining about what you don't have. Would you please think about my limits as a spiritual challenge for you?"

Children who are demanding and grow up with unchecked selfishness will have a harder time as they grow older. They won't have the character necessary to understand and accept the limits that God may place on them. As you help your children address their arguing, badgering, and whining, you will begin to prepare them for a life of contentment. We all need to learn to live within boundaries, whether they are financial limits or health restrictions. Limits are a part of life. Contentment means that we say no to things we can't afford or shouldn't eat. If children can't accept no from their parents, how will they ever learn to say no to themselves or accept limits from God? In the school of life, the "Developing Contentment Curriculum" is not an elective; it's a required course.

We've identified several ways to teach children contentment. The following four strategies help children learn to live within limits, accept a no answer, and develop the character necessary to enjoy life within boundaries.

1. Decrease Emotional Investment

Some children invest a tremendous amount of emotional energy in a request. When it's denied, they experience a major loss. We helped one young man, Daniel, age thirteen, to understand the concept of emotional investment with the following dialogue:

"What is something you'd really like to have?"

"A dog. Not just any dog. I want a yellow Lab."

"How much does one cost?"

"My parents say I need about $500."

"How much money do you have?"

"I have about $400 in my bank account and about $10 more in my drawer at home, so I almost have the money I need."

"Imagine with me for a moment that someone came into your room and stole the $10 out of your drawer. How would you feel?"

"I'd feel bad. I don't like losing money."

"How would you feel if you went to the bank and they told you that someone stole all your money out of your account?"

"I'd feel terrible. I spent a long time saving that money. I worked all last year to save it up. That would make me really mad."

"I can see why that would make you angry. Why would you get more angry when losing the bank account than when losing what's in your drawer?"

"Because it's a lot more money, that's why."

"You're right. Now let's apply this to the times you get angry at home. You seem to be very upset when you get a no answer from Mom. I think it's because you have a lot invested in the request. When you think about it, you're treating some of your drawer requests like bank account issues. Why make it such a big thing to ask for a snack or to go over to a friend's house? Ask yourself why you want it so badly. Why not invest less, leaving yourself alternatives and leaving the door open for a no answer?"

"How do you do that?"

"Maybe you could bring the request to your mom in the idea stage instead of in the final draft. Ideas are more easily changed. Some kids make the final decision and then come for permission, making themselves particularly vulnerable. If they invest less emotion, they can accept no as a redirection instead of a wall." Daniel took our suggestion to heart.

A week later we saw Daniel again and asked him how he was doing with his anger.

"The investment idea helps a lot. I don't get as angry when my mom says no."

"What's your secret? What made it work for you?"

"I realized I don't like losing money and I don't like it when Mom says no, so I decided I would keep less money in my request so I have less to lose."

One mom shared this idea of emotional investment with her four-year-old daughter, Riley. She used a number scale to explain the intensity she saw in her daughter.

"Riley, let's talk about how you ask for things you want," she began. "When you want something very badly, it's like a big number ten." Mom held her arms out wide. "When you want things just a little bit, it's like a little number one," she said, showing about an inch between her thumb and first finger. "If I'm waiting to open a birthday present, it may feel like a number ten!" she continued enthusiastically. "But if I decide to open the mail before I start to cook dinner, that's like a number one."

"I think that sometimes you act like everything you want is a number ten, when really some things should be a two or three…" Mom continued to role-play with Riley some situations that should vary in emotional investment. They had fun with the idea and were able to refer back to the number scale when Riley needed to adjust her intensity.

The idea of emotional investment comes from the apostle Paul's writing when he makes some very important statements about his own life and investments: "But whatever was to my profit I now consider loss for the sake of Christ. What is more, I consider everything a loss compared to the surpassing greatness of knowing Christ Jesus my Lord, for whose sake I have lost all things. I consider them rubbish, that I may gain Christ" (Philippians 3:7-8).

Of course, Paul was much more mature than many adults we know, let alone our children. Yet that passage becomes significant for us, as parents, as we evaluate our own emotional investments. Some parents enter into the arguments because they want to win, show themselves to have more answers, or put a child in his place. Those motivations may reveal some of our own need to reinvest our emotions in godly directions.

Contentment means that we invest less emotion in the things that don't really matter in the end. In fact, learning to accept a no answer is a faith-building exercise and recognizes that the things you want the most may not be the best. As a parent, you can use the daily experiences of life to teach your children about trusting in God. Whether they understand it or not, your goal isn't just to get through the day. You are trying to make decisions now that will help your child get through life successfully.

2. Obey First and Then We'll Talk About It

Children sometimes use arguing, badgering, or whining as delay tactics when they don't like what you ask them to do. Some parents make the mistake of engaging in too much dialogue before a child responds. A second way to develop contentment in children is to teach them to "obey first and then we'll talk about it." Consider this conversation between Julie and her six-year-old, Nathan:

Mom: Nathan, it's time for bed. Please go get your pajamas on.

Nathan: But I don't want to go to bed.

Mom: Nathan, it's 8:00 and you have school tomorrow. You have to go to bed.

Nathan: I'm not tired. I need to finish this house first.

Mom: What are you doing?

Nathan: I'm building a Lego village and working on this house.

Mom: No, you can work on it tomorrow. If you don't get to bed, you won't be able to get up in the morning.

Nathan: I won't be tired tomorrow.

Mom: Nathan, it's time to go to bed.

Nathan: But Mooommm!

Mom: What?!

Nathan: Can't I just stay up a little longer? I'm almost done.

Mom: How long?

Nathan: I don't know, just a few minutes.

Mom: All right, I'll let you stay up until 8:15. No later. Then you need to go to bed.

Nathan: Okay.

(Round Two began at 8:15.)

Julie knows her son needs sleep, but she's reluctant to push past all the whining, badgering, and arguing from Nathan.

Here's a different scenario:

Mom: Nathan, it's time to go get on your pajamas.

Nathan: But I don't want to go to bed.

Mom: Nathan, you need to obey first, and then we'll talk about it. It's 7:45 and you need to get on your pajamas now.

Nathan: But I'm not tired…

Mom: Nathan, I'm not having a discussion until you obey. First you do what I said, and then we'll talk about it. Please go get on your pajamas now.

Nathan: All right.

Although having discussions with children is generally a good idea, it's often counterproductive in the instruction process. Parents sometimes try to talk their children into obeying, or they believe they need to explain all the reasons why a child should obey the request.

The fact is that, even as adults, we sometimes need to obey without knowing the whole story. You may not understand why your boss has given a certain assignment. You do it and discover why later. You may drive down a road and come to a policeman who is redirecting traffic. You don't roll down the window and have a discussion with him. You follow directions and maybe learn more later. You don't understand, but you do it anyway. God sometimes asks people to obey before they understand why. Noah spent over one hundred years building a boat before he ever saw rain. Abraham was asked to leave his family and homeland to go to a new land that he had never been to before.

Remember, the goal is to develop contentment in our children. Sometimes it's best for our kids to put their agenda aside for someone else or learn to live with their second choice instead of always expecting life to go their way.

Interestingly enough, often children don't want to talk about it after the fact. This further demonstrates that the kids are not so much concerned with the answers as they are with getting what they want when they want it. When possible, talk about it afterwards and discuss the hows and whys of your requests or no answers. Your kids may not agree or even understand, but the discussions provide opportunities to teach them about values.

Following someone else's leadership develops trust and teaches children how to follow God's leading as they get older. Some children are so self-centered that they always have to lead. They expect parents to convince them of the benefit of doing something before they are willing to do it. These children grow up to be poor employees, have bad attitudes about following someone else's leadership, and have a difficult time in relationships. When you teach your children to obey first and then talk about it, you are preparing them for a life of following God as they grow older.

3. Offer a Wise Appeal

Giving children a way to appeal can be very helpful and actually equips them with a life-long skill. Not all kids can handle it, but you'd be surprised at what happens when you add a wise appeal to your interaction. It not only gives your children an alternative, but it teaches them an honoring way to present ideas to those in authority with whom they disagree.

In order to teach your kids about the wise appeal, you might begin with having them learn this formula:

I understand you want me to…because…
I have a problem with that because…
So could I please…

All three phrases have a purpose. The first one helps a child identify with the parent's wishes. Trevor, age seven, might say, "I understand you want me to clean up the playroom because we're going out to run errands." It's amazing how easy it is to listen to alternatives once we, as parents, feel understood. We all want people to understand us; giving the gift of understanding paves the way for real listening, and even negotiation, to take place.

The second statement allows a child to express the problem or objection. Trevor may continue with, "I have a problem with that because I just set up my train track and I haven't even run the trains around it yet." This statement allows the parent to hear the problem without a whining or otherwise irritating approach.

The third statement provides a creative alternative that tries to take both the parent's concern and the child's wishes into account. "So could I please leave it out and play with it when we get back?" The child has offered an alternative instead of just dumping a problem on Mom or Dad.

The wise appeal requires some maturity and often takes work for a parent to teach it, but those who spend the extra energy give their kids a valuable skill. Instead of whining, badgering, or arguing, children learn how to bring about change and do it with an attitude of cooperation instead of antagonism.

In fact, we have seen parents teach the wise appeal to children as young as three years old. They do this with a "fill in the blank" approach. The parent says the first part, and the child learns to fill in the blank. When your child is ready, don't be afraid of the wise appeal. Use it to teach children how to dialogue about issues at appropriate times and in a wise way. It's a routine that will help them to initiate change by considering the other person in the process.

Of course, it's important for a child who presents a wise appeal to be able to still accept no for an answer. When children can't accept no, they need to go back to "Obey first and then we'll talk about it." Furthermore, the wise appeal can't be used as a delay tactic just to get out of a job. If Trevor doesn't really intend to play with the train when he gets home, he has misused the wise appeal and may lose the privilege of using it. The wise appeal becomes an unwritten contract between parent and child and is available only to children who are responsible with it.

The Scriptures tell us about making a wise appeal in the stories of Daniel, Esther, and Nehemiah. Each individual had to go to an authority with a request, and they each received a positive answer, in part, because of the way they appealed. The wise appeal is not a magic formula, but you'd be surprised at how often it works. It would be nice if more adults would learn the wise appeal instead of just going about life whining or complaining.

Keith faced an interesting problem during his first year of college. He was disappointed with the school's lack of initiative in getting students involved in community service. He felt that community involvement would be a helpful way for students to take what they learned in class and integrate it into real life. Instead of just criticizing or complaining about the problem, Keith created a written wise appeal and took it to his faculty advisor. The faculty advisor liked what he saw and asked Keith to share the idea with the other professors at their next meeting. The faculty saw some value in what Keith was sharing and asked him to present his ideas to the student body. In the coming weeks Keith worked alongside his faculty advisor to help make community service projects available to the students who were interested. Keith used a wise appeal to initiate change in his college environment.

The child who uses the wise appeal learns that when she approaches a parent in a wise and honoring way, she can trust her parent to listen and consider what's best for her. After a wise appeal, a child still needs to accept a parent's answer and be content with it. The child gives up control. This sets the stage to teach the child to bring requests to God through prayer but be willing to trust God with the answer.

Imagine Jesus in the Garden of Gethsemane, praying on the

night he was arrested. He came to his Father with an appeal. In Luke 22:42 we read Jesus' words: "Father, if you are willing, take this cup from me; yet not my will, but yours be done." Humanly speaking, he asked for another alternative than the one he was facing. Jesus received a no answer, but his ultimate goal, even in the appeal, was to trust God fully.

The wise appeal replaces complaining and whining with trust. As you teach it to your children, pray that God will develop contentment in them.

4. Abandon Manipulative Techniques

Much of the whining, badgering, and arguing that children use works. Too often parents give in or engage with their kids. Don't do it. Refuse to play the same old games. Instead, gently redirect the conversation or set firm limits on your child's demandingness. You may need to give a consequence or remove a privilege. Remember though, the goal is not punishment by dishing out a sentence for misbehavior. The goal is discipline, redirecting your child's energies into healthy alternatives.

One dad wanted to address arguing with his eleven-year-old daughter. He sat down and explained that he wasn't going to carry on the same kind of conversations anymore because their relating patterns were hurting the relationship, not helping it. "Leslie, I feel uncomfortable about the arguments we have. I want to change the way we discuss things. Before you disagree or give me another alternative, I'd like you to first affirm the last thing I said, and I'll do the same for you." Dad looked for ways to affirm Leslie's statements. He gently reminded her each time she was tempted to launch into an argument. When Leslie wanted to go over to a friend's house on family-housecleaning day, for instance, her dad might tell her, "I understand you want to go to your friend's house. That sounds like fun, but today is not a good day for it." Affirming the previous statement was enough to take the edge off their strained relationship. They were then able to have helpful and interesting conversations together.

Teach your kids what they should do when they want something. Role-play responses that emphasize contentment and gratefulness. When you are about to give a no answer, slow down the process for your children and warn them that a challenge is coming.

One of my (Joanne) sons struggled in this area of disappointment when he was young. I saw a pattern that concerned me. When I had to say no to his request, he typically became angry and retreated in silence. Sometimes he would bang or kick, other times he would bury his head in the sofa. He refused to talk but would withdraw with a scowl. These behaviors demonstrated demandingness and an inability to handle disappointment. There was no arguing or badgering, but the problem was clear. Over time we addressed this issue from several angles. My husband and I made observations and gently discussed the problem with our son so that he could see it. We talked about anger management skills and practiced them. We also talked about emotional investment and contentment, pointing out a need to develop flexibility. As our son grew in his awareness and ability to deal with the problem, I would sometimes warn him before I gave an answer to his request. "Are you ready for an answer? Can you accept a yes or a no?" By preparing him before the answer, I was able to slow down the process and help him make the necessary adjustments in his heart.

THE BETTER RESPONSE

Many adults haven't learned how to accept no as an answer. They become critical and act just like kids who whine and complain. When demandingness comes out in your kids, you have an opportunity to teach a better response.

Paul challenged the Philippians to "do everything without

complaining or arguing" (Philippians 2:14). A child's negative techniques often work, but the child gets a yes answer at a cost. Parents who try to keep the peace by giving in to arguing, badgering, or whining inadvertently encourage selfish behavior. Recognize the need to address these problems in a healthy way and implement the "Developing Contentment Curriculum." We want our kids to develop contentment, because when they do, they will be able to enjoy life within the limits God sets for them.

PUTTING IT ALL TOGETHER

When You See…
Whining, complaining, arguing, and badgering, view them as flags that reveal demandingness.

Move into a Routine…
That changes the way you relate. Look at the patterns that have developed and identify the specific places where healthy dialogue turns hurtful. Teach children to accept a no answer by understanding emotional investment, learning to obey first and then talk about it, offering a wise appeal, and abandoning their manipulative techniques.

Because…
Teaching children to accept limits helps them learn contentment. Faith in God starts with our ability to trust him instead of becoming demanding with others.

QUESTIONS FOR FURTHER DISCUSSION

1. Give an example of something you've had to give up as an act of faith because pursuing it would be hurtful to your

relationship with others. You just couldn't push any further without hurting people.

2. Name a time when you as an adult had to obey first and then talk about it afterwards. This might be an experience with a boss or other authority or an experience with God.

3. How can you tell when you're becoming demanding with others? What are the symptoms that start raising your awareness that it's time to back off?

DIGGING DEEPER

1. Read Philippians 4:12. The apostle Paul was intense about his objectives and goals as he did missionary work. How can you, like Paul, be content yet pursue goals in life? Are those two concepts contradictory?

2. Read 1 Timothy 6:6-11. Why do you think God considers contentment to be such a valuable quality in life?

3. Read Luke 18:1-8. Jesus encourages persistence in prayer. How is persistence different from badgering?

BRINGING IT HOME

Go to your local library and check out a book or two about badgers. As a family, discuss the characteristics and habits of these animals. What qualities do they possess? Ask your children to name positive and negative results from acting similar to a badger.

6

Your attitude should be the same as that of Christ Jesus.

PHILIPPIANS 2:5

"They Always Grumble and Complain"

Attitude:

Giving the Gift of Perspective

Dear Scott and Joanne,

The thing that frustrates me the most in parenting is my kids' attitude. When I suggest that my ten-year-old son, Matthew, invite a friend over, he says, "I'm no good at talking on the phone." When I ask him to finish mowing around the flowerbed, he says, "I'll never get it right." Whenever I ask him to do anything around the house, he says things like "I always have to work" or "I'll never get this done." We have such a hard time with home-work. He says, "I hate this. When will I ever use this stuff? This is such a waste of time."

Before attending your seminar, it had never occurred to me to discipline for a bad attitude. Now I see how important that is. I've started enforcing what I call an "attitude break." Matthew now knows that if he starts with a bad attitude, then I'm going to have him sit for a few minutes, or longer if necessary, until he can come back and make a positive statement before we continue. We've got a long way to go, but I'm very pleased with the progress we've made in the past few weeks. He's responding pretty well to this approach. I've even heard him correct himself sometimes without the break. I realize now that I need to address his bad attitude or he's going to grow up to be an unhappy person.

—Tom from Dallas, Texas

"But Moooom!"

We've all heard it: the bad attitude that so quickly jumps out when kids are disappointed or we ask them to do something they don't want to do. Bad attitudes are not only irritating to parents, but they also tend to grow worse if we don't challenge them.

Not all bad attitudes are the same. Some children have an attitude of demandingness: "I want it and I want it now!" Others have an attitude of inferiority: "I'll never get it right." Others put on a victim attitude: "I always get the worst part." And then there's the common "I hate school" attitude or the "My brother is less than human" attitude.

One mom told us, "I just thought one attitude was the same as another. I now see that sometimes my daughter has a defiant attitude with me and other times a prideful attitude with her friends. Seeing different kinds of bad attitudes has helped me target my comments as I work with her."

God is concerned about attitude because it's an expression of the heart. Attitudes help determine how a person responds to life and its challenges. Jesus criticized the Pharisees because of their hypocritical attitude (Luke 13:15). A prideful attitude almost prevented Naaman from receiving healing of his leprosy (2 Kings 5:11-12). And when Sarah was told she would have a child, her little snicker indicated an attitude of disbelief that caused God to question her faith (Genesis 18:12-15).

On the other hand, when Jesus saw the attitude of the centurion whose servant was dying, he affirmed him by saying, "I have not found such great faith even in Israel" (Luke 7:9). The prodigal son had a humble attitude and returned to the blessing of his father (Luke 15:19). God knows what attitudes will bring success, and he teaches us how to face life's challenges with a mind-set focused on him. God encourages humility instead of pride (Matthew 23:11-12), joy when facing trials (James 1:2), gentleness when confronting others (Galatians 6:1), and an attitude of hope when circumstances are discouraging (Romans 5:5). The person who has these attitudes can enjoy life and experience more peace and fulfillment.

As you help your children change their attitudes, you will give them a new perspective on life. They will learn to see their grumbling and complaining as choices they're making. It's been said, "You can change your attitude in one moment and, in that moment, change the course of your whole day." Bad attitudes are a common problem and shouldn't be overlooked. When children learn to address their attitudes, they learn to gain control of their emotional responses and are able to think rightly about life's challenges.

WHAT IS AN ATTITUDE?

"Attitude" is a shorthand term used to summarize many different feelings, thoughts, and behaviors all at the same time. An attitude describes a person's tendency to act the same way each time a particular situation comes about. Various triggers provoke attitudes. Simply hearing a word or seeing a sign can change a person's perspective. All Mom has to do is say "Derek" with that certain voice, for instance, and Derek knows she is going to ask him to do something. He responds with "Yeah, whadaya want?" Victoria gets to school and sees a pink slip taped to her locker again. She doesn't even read it but rolls her eyes and groans knowing that it's a call to the office. Triggers like

These quotes about attitude might be helpful for you and your kids:

- "Life is 10 percent what happens to you and 90 percent attitude."
- "Ability is what you're capable of doing. Motivation determines what you do. Attitude determines how well you do it." —Lou Holtz
- "Our attitude toward life determines life's attitude towards us." —Earl Nightingale
- "Whether a glass is half full or half empty depends on the attitude of the person looking at it."
- "Where the heart is willing, it will find a thousand ways. Where it is unwilling, it will find a thousand excuses." —Arlen Price
- "If you don't learn to laugh at troubles, you won't have anything to laugh at when you grow old." —Ed Howe
- "Pain is inevitable, but misery is optional." —Barbara Johnson
- "Your attitude is contagious. Is yours worth catching?"
- "Attitude, not aptitude, determines your altitude."
- "Attitude is a little thing that makes a BIG difference. An optimist sees an opportunity in every calamity, a pessimist sees calamity in every opportunity."
  —Winston Churchill

these quickly move people into attitudes that help determine how they will respond to a situation.

Attitudes can be good or bad and are inherently interwoven into everything we do. They often rest just below the surface and are sometimes difficult to read or understand in adults, let alone in our children. Billions of advertising dollars are spent each year to create or change attitudes in you toward certain products or activities. Cancer research and prevention groups pay for billboards to develop negative attitudes toward smoking. Car manufacturers try to create in you a positive attitude toward their latest vehicles, and advertisers spend big bucks to convince preschoolers that a particular breakfast cereal is the best. They do all of this to influence attitudes because attitudes change behavior. Furthermore, attitudes are highly contagious. As a parent, you know that children can develop a whole outlook on life based on the latest television show or by spending time with a particular friend. Attitudes affect how we view life and respond to it.

You can never get rid of attitudes, nor would you want to. You can only change them. Attitudes are a way of thinking about certain aspects of life. They actually have a purpose: to prepackage a response based on a history of similar experiences. Attitudes help people understand the world and make sense of the things around them. They are necessary shortcuts and provide consistency and clarity for knowing how to respond to repeated events and situations. Without attitudes, you would have to reevaluate each person, food, and entertainment choice over and over again, making life unbearably complicated. Instead, your attitude prepares your posture and gives you a pattern of response every time you see a familiar trigger.

Take a moment and think about Dunkin' Donuts, roller coasters, motorcycle gangs, and your church. No doubt those words conjure up various attitudes based on your personal experience. Compare that to your attitude toward the people of Vambonia. Since you've never heard of Vambonians (we just made up that name), you will have little or no attitude toward them. However, if we were to give you one piece of information, say that they hate children, you would begin to develop an attitude about them. Attitudes come from your experience and help determine how you will respond. They give insight into your values and beliefs.

Children tend to develop simplistic attitudes about life based on limited information. Your eight-year-old son may have a bad attitude about vegetables because he doesn't like the taste of peas. You, however, may choose to eat a variety of vegetables for very different reasons. Your attitude toward vegetables takes many more pieces of information into account and gives you a different mind-set toward them.

Certain attitudes about style, music, sports, and current fads often come from a child's friends. Media, movies, and even commercials contribute greatly to children's attitudes about the foods they like to eat and their opinions about romantic relationships. The family also has a tremendous influence on attitudes, especially for young children. Kids often copy their parents' attitudes toward faith, work, and habits like smoking, drinking, and taking drugs. Attitudes are learned in a variety of different contexts, but one doesn't always have to pick them up from an outside source. We are all basically selfish, and sometimes a bad attitude is simply an outward reflection of the selfishness in our own hearts.

What does God say about what an "attitude" is? The Bible translators came to an interesting dilemma as they worked on the New Testament. Sometimes where the *King James Version* uses the word "mind" the *New International Version* translates it as "attitude." Note the following verses:

Philippians 2:5

Your *attitude* should be the same as that of Christ Jesus. (NIV, emphasis added)

Let this *mind* be in you, which was also in Christ Jesus.
(KJV, emphasis added)

1 Peter 4:1

Therefore, since Christ suffered in his body, arm yourselves
also with the same *attitude.* (NIV, emphasis added)

Forasmuch then as Christ hath suffered for us in the flesh,
arm yourselves likewise with the same *mind.* (KJV, emphasis
added)

Both translations are accurate. The Greek word used in those passages refers to a frame of mind or a mind-set to act in a particular way.
Christians are to have a way of thinking and responding to life that
mirrors that of Jesus Christ. This is a perspective we want to pass on
to our children.

ATTITUDES RUN DEEP

Attitudes become the grid through which we see the world. The way
you teach your children now about attitudes can set the stage for them
to understand how to have godly perspectives in difficult situations as
they grow older.

Attitudes actually have three components: acting, feeling, and
thinking. Each one is useful in the change process. The behavior is a
flag to see the problem and know *where* to target the change. The
emotion helps you know *when* to correct, and the thinking shows you
what you need to address. Many parents only focus on the first one,
behavior, telling kids, "Quit pouting" or "Don't roll your eyes at me."
Furthermore, these parents tend to focus only on what not to do
instead of what the child *should* do. It usually isn't helpful just to tell
a child to "Stop having a bad attitude" without giving more guidance

for developing a better response. If the bad attitude is coming from a thinking error, behavior change is not enough.

Remember that the goal of discipline is not just to make your children less annoying. As you correct your children for bad attitudes, you are preparing them for the future. If their grumbling and complaining is stirring up anger in you, use that anger as a flag that it's time to help your kids develop a new perspective.

Behavior: The Warning Flag

The first component of a bad attitude is behavior: the things we do. Habits of walking, talking, standing, looking, ignoring, or engaging often reveal what the heart is thinking and feeling. Now, you may be asking, "If the real issue is in the heart, what am I supposed to do about the behavior?" The answer has two parts. First, we use the behavior to indicate that we need to look deeper and address the attitudes of the heart. Second, we correct the wrong behavior. Although we can't force a change of heart, we can require that children change their behavior while we continue to talk about heart-level changes.

Use behavior as a warning flag. Identify how your child tends to show a bad attitude and point out the patterns of behavior you see: "I can tell you're disappointed by the way you're rolling your eyes, but that's not an acceptable way to treat others just because you're unhappy." "Those comments are hurtful and reflect a bad attitude because I said no." "I can tell by your posture and sad face that you don't want to do what I asked you to do, but that kind of bad attitude is not helpful."

Sometimes the cues are subtle and other times glaringly obvious. When you give an instruction, for example, does your child make eye contact and give an appropriate response? Or does your child respond with arguing, complaining, anger, and defensiveness? Look at body language too. Huffing, folded arms, and rolling eyes demonstrate a message. Did the child do the task willingly, or was it done grudgingly, with bickering or complaining? Did your son do a complete and thorough job, or did he do it poorly, part way, or slowly? Did your daughter report back to have the work checked when she was finished, or did she disappear and you had to go find her?

Your answers to these questions may indicate a problem. Maybe the issue isn't an attitude problem; maybe it's a character weakness such as distractibility or laziness. Either way, children need to learn what their behavior, or lack of it, is saying to others.

Correct your child with clear observations of what you see. "I can tell you're upset by the way you're raising your voice. I'd like you to take a break before this gets out of hand." Or, "Thank you for doing what I asked you to do. I appreciate that, but did you notice how you responded when I gave you the instruction? You clicked your tongue and let out a deep breath that sent a message that you didn't like it. That's a hurtful response."

One mom used picture words when her children were young to help them see their attitude. Words like "cloudy," "dark," "mean-faced," "scowling," or "pouting" referred to a bad attitude. "Bubbly," "sunshine," or a smiling heart revealed a good attitude. Another mom encouraged her children to put on a good attitude with their clothes in the morning and check the mirror to make sure it was on straight. "Not only do you put on an attitude, but you leave one wherever you go," she would say.

Children often don't realize what their actions are communicating. Pointing out actual behaviors and connecting these to the attitude can be helpful. Your goal is to help children see their own warning signals and make adjustments accordingly. Help them see that it's time for an attitude tune-up.

Emotion: The Guide to Timing

The second component of an attitude is emotion. Sensitivity to a child's emotions helps a parent know *when* to challenge the attitude. Sometimes it's best to do it right on the spot. Children who are generally quiet, withdrawn, or unmotivated may suddenly be willing to talk when something triggers their emotions.

On the other hand, children who are already intense about life may go over the edge if you challenge them in the midst of an emotional experience. In that situation, a sensitive parent realizes that confronting about attitude on the spot may escalate the conflict. You may choose to confront the child later, after the emotion has subsided.

A bad attitude is often anger in disguise. The child, who doesn't like an instruction or limitation, reveals frustration outwardly, sometimes in a small way and other times with downright revenge. One mom said, "I can tell when my thirteen-year-old son is having a bad attitude. He becomes more abrupt in his actions and words. His roughness yells a message that says, 'I'm not happy with you.'"

It's important to remember two rules of engagement when considering a child's emotions.

Rule of Engagement 1: Don't Be Afraid of Your Child's Emotions

Sometimes children use an outburst as a form of self-protection to prevent parents from challenging them. Your child may react like a volcano, but don't let that stop you from your job of correcting and confronting. View the emotion as a smoke screen and look past it to the heart of the issue. Parents too often see the emotion as a personal attack and react to it, losing any real benefit that could come from the interaction. That brings us to…

Rule of Engagement 2: Don't Use Your Own Anger to Overpower Your Child's Anger

Remember that you're trying to help your child think differently and respond in a healthier way. When you respond with anger, you communicate a mixed message. Your children now need to not only sort out right and wrong thinking about life, but they must also tiptoe around your harshness. This confuses kids and actually prevents them from dealing with their own part of the problem.

Proverbs 15:1 says, "A gentle answer turns away wrath." Your anger may be pointing out a problem, but be careful how you react. Remain calm and in control in response to your child's grumbling and complaining. When you begin to lose it, take a break. Bad attitudes are addressed over time anyway; we can only get so much out of each situation. Come back later and work on it some more: "I've been thinking about the way you responded to me earlier when I asked you to do your homework. I'd like to share an observation that might be helpful for you. It seems that you believe you ought to be able to wait and do your homework just before bed or in the morning before you go to school. Is that what you're saying? One of the values I'm trying to teach you is that self-discipline often means we work first and play later. That's one of the reasons I require you to do your homework early every day. I'm trying to teach you an important value. I know that you may not agree with me, but I want you to know why I'm asking you to do homework before dinner."

Allowing emotions to settle first can bring opportunities for dialogue later, instead of turning the present issue into a battleground. You don't have to feel like you've won in a confrontation in order to make progress. Realize that kids will go away thinking about what you've said, even if their initial response looks as if they haven't heard you. This is especially true for teenagers. Prepare what you're going to say and choose your timing carefully without getting caught up in the emotion of the moment.

Some parents believe that they must be consistent and correct on the spot every time they see the problem. That is not always true about an attitude. The emotional component sometimes suggests that you wait until later.

Thinking: The Heart of the Issue

An attitude tune-up ultimately addresses the mind: how children think and what they believe. An attitude is a mind-set. Attitudes reflect how we process information and experiences. When an actor dressed in a white lab coat tells you that one particular toothpaste is the best because it fights cavities, you may believe him and have a positive attitude toward that toothpaste, even though all toothpaste fights cavities. When a friend tells your teenage daughter that her shoes are out of style, you may try to convince her otherwise by showing her the latest catalogs, but she will choose whom she wishes to believe and develop an attitude toward shoe styles accordingly.

To help your children develop right thinking patterns, start by identifying the thinking errors that may be leading to a bad attitude. Here are a few:

"Work is a disruption to my fun in life."

"I should be able to do what I want to do."

"My parents shouldn't be correcting me for this kind of thing."

"My parents are too strict."

"My brother has problems too, but he never gets in trouble."

Take time to ask questions about your child's bad attitude to find what error may lie behind it. Dialogue with your child to get at some of those hidden issues. Be careful if the discussion becomes emotionally charged. Although meanness should be a signal that the conversation needs a break, don't be overly put off by a child's intensity. When your child speaks strongly, you may gain insight into some underlying beliefs. Children sometimes say things in anger that they wouldn't normally say. These statements are clues to thinking errors. You don't want to try to reason with your child when he's angry, but listen and then you'll be able to discuss the issues later. After a break, come back with questions, suggestions, and statements of right thinking, and continue to dialogue.

The goal is to help children think rightly, and that takes time. Questions like "Why do you think that's unfair?" or "Tell me how I could have handled it differently?" can often help kids get started. Your persistence will pay off as you try to help replace the lies or immaturity with healthy statements that they can say to themselves.

Having discussions with your child may seem contrary to what you've learned about discipline and training. After all, children need to learn how to obey without a dialogue and learn to respect authority without continually challenging it. Even in this book we've talked about teaching children to "obey first and then we'll talk about it" as a way to address a problem like whining and complaining. These approaches emphasize the need for children to respond to authority, give up their agendas, and learn cooperation. We encourage you to continue with those techniques because they teach kids valuable things about life, but don't stop there.

Dialogue helps you understand your child so you know what to emphasize and how to teach it effectively. The older the child, the more necessary dialogue becomes in the teaching process. Unfortunately, as kids go through their teen years, it's harder to initiate these types of conversations with them. Teens may not be interested in dialoguing when you want to talk. In this case, you need to be on the lookout for conversation starters. They may begin with a simple observation from you or your child. Prepare yourself for the unexpected discussion so you'll be able to take advantage of those teachable moments.

Listening carefully to your child can help you identify thinking errors that lead to a bad attitude. What hidden belief might Jeremy, age ten, have? He complains and argues when you ask him to do the dishes. Maybe he believes "Chores are an interruption to my life." If pressed, he may also reveal this belief: "All work is hard and unpleasant, and I must try to avoid it." A positive attitude about work comes from several new values such as "Work is necessary in order to bring benefits to me and to others" or "My contribution to family life is a statement of gratefulness for what I have."

Scriptures That Communicate Right Thinking

- The value of hard work: Proverbs 6:6-9 and 14:23
- The value of correction: Proverbs 12:1
- The value of listening to instruction: Proverbs 1:8-9 and 4:1
- The value of humility: Proverbs 18:12
- The value of obedience: Ephesians 6:1-2
- The value of doing good to those who offend you: Romans 12:18-21
- The value of contentment: 1 Timothy 6:6
- The value of overlooking an offense: Matthew 5:39-45
- The value of bringing peace instead of conflict: Matthew 5:9
- The value of hospitality: Hebrews 13:2
- The value of controlling anger: James 1:20

When Dad sees Christina, age eight, wearing the same dirty shirt three days in a row, he may correct her and tell her to change it. Christina's grumbling response on the way to her room is a bad attitude and may reflect a belief that "I should be able to decide what I want to wear." If pressed, Christina may also hold to the idea that "correction is a personal attack; therefore, I must defend myself at all cost." Christina needs to say different things to herself such as "My Dad sees something I don't see. I need to listen to him and try to understand why he's saying it."

When seven-year-old Anthony is told that he can't go to his friend's house until he picks up his toys in the living room, his mean words to Mom reveal a bad attitude. This may come from the belief that "a neat living room is not important," or worse yet, "Mom is just being selfish because she wants me to clean up the living room." Anthony needs to learn a positive attitude toward instruction. He could say to himself, "I can be flexible and go in a little while" or "Just because I don't like a request doesn't mean I can treat my mom unkindly."

The opinions and beliefs that children hold are important, and to change them requires heavy doses of dialogue, parental vulnerability, patience, and love. At first, you may choose long breaks between an offense and the correction just so you have time to figure out what's going on, think about what the wrong beliefs might be, and then develop a wise plan.

Remember that overpowering kids may change behavior but it does little good for changing anyone's mind. Use creativity and consistency instead to influence the way your children think. You might have them write positive things to say when they're disappointed and maybe even read those positive thoughts out loud to transform negative thinking. Hebrews 4:12 says that the Word of God is able to judge the "thoughts and attitudes of the heart." Teach your kids that the Scriptures are a powerful force for change, and choose strategic

Bible verses to memorize. Pray for and with your children specifically about attitude. You may also make attitude posters to put up around the house or little reminder cards to encourage right thinking. Pay attention to the friends, media, and activities that influence your children, realizing that attitudes are more often caught than taught. Remember that God is interested in your child's heart, and you are partnering with him to help your children develop godly attitudes about life.

AN EXPERIMENT ON YOU

Pause and think for a minute. What is your attitude toward bad attitudes? If this chapter is successful, you'll begin to see some attitude changes in yourself. Evaluate your own heart. Ask yourself what triggers a bad attitude in you. When your daughter pouts or your son complains, how do you respond? Your angry tone of voice may be the symptom of a bad attitude. Maybe your belief goes something similar to this: "I don't ask him to do much at all. He's so ungrateful." When pressed you may also believe, "My son's bad attitude makes my life hard. I hate the resistance he always gives me." It's possible that you have developed a bad attitude about bad attitudes. What you need is an attitude tune-up.

What reactions should you have when you see a bad attitude? How about this one: "Oh good, I'm getting a window into my son's heart. It looks like he must have some wrong thinking that needs to be addressed. I need to think about this and figure out what's really going on."

It certainly would be a lot easier if your kids appreciated your correction, instruction, and limitations, wouldn't it? One mom said, "Just once I'd like to hear my daughter thank me for making her clean her room." Unfortunately, it doesn't usually happen that way. Kids would learn faster and you'd have less work and frustration if it did, but raising children isn't that easy. Even Solomon himself must have recognized this problem because over twenty-five times in the book of Proverbs he reminds children and young people to listen to instructions, rebukes, and warnings.

Expect resistance. It's part of the job. Learn to relate in those times without anger. A bad attitude needs to be addressed, but not with anger. Sometimes children put up the greatest resistance when they need correction the most. Let that grumbling or pouting be a flag that it's time to correct some thinking errors and give your child a new perspective.

So, is it working? Is your attitude changing as you think about bad attitudes? We hope so. Your work at changing your own attitude will not only give you insight into the process of change, but it will improve your relationship with your children as well.

HOW DO I DO IT?

Helping children change bad attitudes isn't easy. It takes time and planning to develop right thinking. When you see behavior that indicates an attitude problem, consider the situation and try to determine how best to influence your children toward healthier patterns. Here are several ways you can target thinking errors that lead to bad attitudes.

1. Help Children Express Themselves in Healthy Ways

Self-awareness isn't high on the list of strengths for most kids. It's hard to adjust thinking errors if children don't even know what they're thinking and feeling. Of course, some children are harder to read than others. If you ask them, "What are you thinking?" they may not know. In fact, "I don't know" and "Nothing" are two common answers from children.

Mom: How was your day?

Son: I don't know.

Mom: What did you do?

Son: Nothing.

Mom: Did you do anything fun in school today?

Son: I don't know.

Mom: What did you learn?

Son: Nothing.

Mom: What would you like for dinner?

Son: I don't know.

When you hear these answers, don't just go on. Instead, look for ways to draw your children out. "Tell me one story about school today." Reflect the feelings they might be experiencing. "That sounds frustrating" or "I'll bet that made you feel pretty good." These comments can help children recognize the feelings that are contributing to their attitudes.

When toddlers and preschoolers are learning how to talk, you help them communicate what they want. You may say to your two-year-old, "Do you want the ball? Don't scream. Say, 'Ball please.'" You teach them to verbalize what they're thinking. In the same way, older children may not have the emotional vocabulary to communicate what they believe or feel. You can help them by talking about different beliefs and drawing out what is going on inside. You may say to your nine-year-old, "I can tell you're unhappy by your tone of voice. It sounds like you believe that my answer was unfair and you're feeling frustrated. Is that true? Let's talk about it instead of mistreating each other."

2. Look for Influences in Your Child's Life That Contribute to a Bad Attitude

One dad said, "I realized that my son tends to have a more aggressive attitude toward me after he's played computer games for awhile. When I took away the games and replaced that time with family reading, I saw improvement." In your family, you may not choose to remove the computer games, but you might talk to your kids about your observation and see if they can make appropriate adjustments. If, however, they can't handle a particular friend, privilege, or type of entertainment, they may need to lose it for a time until they become more mature.

3. Challenge Bad Attitudes Directly

One mom told us, "My son had a terrible attitude that said, 'You have no right to discipline me.' This attitude went on for several weeks before I figured out what was going on. He would tell me to get out of his room, and he resisted instruction or correction. I made the mistake of arguing and fighting with him. When it finally hit me what was happening, we sat down and had a conversation about my role as a parent. He didn't like what I had to say, but I also spent time listening to him. Our conversation was very enlightening for both of us. We even had fun laughing at points. I look back now and see that our discussion that day made all the difference. I was able to identify his thinking errors and have a frank discussion about them. I only wish I could have seen it earlier in the process." Direct conversations such as this help children see that their bad attitudes are a problem and that they need to make changes.

4. Teach Children a Better Way to Respond

Rather than focusing only on the negative, teach children what actions demonstrate a positive attitude. How should children respond when they get an instruction they'd rather not hear? "Okay" is a good place to start. How should a child respond when you correct him? "I'm sorry" or "I was wrong." How should a child respond when she's disappointed with a no answer? "Maybe next time." These responses can actually change the way a child thinks about the instruction, correction, or disappointment.

5. Affirm Progress

Sometimes change takes so long that by the time your children respond well, you're ready to say, "It's about time!" Resist that temptation and affirm the progress your children are making. When you see a positive attitude, point it out. One dad said, "This was the best thing we could do to help our fifteen-year-old daughter, Ashley, change her attitude. I began affirming her when I saw her answer me in a positive way, when she contributed to conversations, smiled, said okay, apologized, or just did what I asked." Affirming her steps of progress encouraged Ashley to keep moving in the right direction.

You may be surprised how well this approach works. After working on her son's poor response to correction for what seemed like months, the mom of a teen warned her son one day that he was heading down a negative path again. "I went into his room and told him what I saw, and his answer floored me. I was speechless. He said, 'Okay, Mom, thanks. I'll take care of it.' I was so pleased, my response of surprise and gratefulness was fun for both of us." This mom affirmed the positive response of her son, and that further encouraged his progress in dealing with his attitude.

6. Help Children See What's Happening

Identifying a thinking error that needs to change may be a new revelation for children who are stuck in a bad attitude. They may be responding to a situation only on an emotional level. You can offer the insight of an objective outsider.

Recognize, too, that not all bad attitudes come from wrong thinking. The child who has a fight with her friend and takes it out on her sister, for instance, may be overwhelmed emotionally. When we're under a lot of stress or feeling hurt about a particular relationship or situation, we sometimes take it out on others. In the same way that cars need gas to fill up their fuel tanks, or cell phones need their batteries recharged, we often need to refill our emotional tanks and recharge our emotional batteries. Where do you go to recharge your emotions? The best place to go is to God. Teach children what this means in practical terms. Getting alone, praying, reading the Bible, and thinking about things you're thankful for can do a lot to change your attitude. Even though an attitude problem may stem from a strong emotional reaction, at least part of the solution is to learn how to think rightly.

Melanie, age sixteen, came home from school with an obvious attitude problem. She yelled at her brother, grumbled when her mom asked her to pick up her things in the living room, and was generally frustrated and angry. An hour or so later, Melanie came into the kitchen to ask when dinner would be ready. Mom chose that time to make some observations about what she saw and to begin a conversation. "Melanie, it looks as if something's bothering you. What's going on?"

"I'm fine. What do you mean?"

"It just seems that you came home from school angry. You had a short fuse with Isaac and grumbled when I asked you to clean up. Is something going on at school?"

"Well, we have a group project due tomorrow, and the other kids aren't helping at all. I'm trying to pull it together so we can get a good grade."

"Oh wow. That's frustrating."

"I'm just tired. The last few nights I've stayed up late, and I really need to get some sleep. I also have my recital this weekend, and I need to work more on my music."

"I can see why you're frustrated. That's a lot of things all at the same time. I can imagine you might feel overwhelmed."

"Yeah. It's a lot."

"It sounds like you need to work hard the next few days, get some more sleep, and just concentrate on pulling through the weekend."

"Hmm, I guess you're right."

"Sometimes when people feel overwhelmed, they imagine that they're stuck and will never get out. After you've been overwhelmed a few times though, you start telling yourself, 'This pressure will pass.' You know what I mean?"

"Yeah, I guess."

"God teaches us all kinds of things under pressure. You might want to pray and ask him to give you the strength and wisdom to get through these next few days."

"Okay."

"I can tell you've got a lot on your mind. I hope, though, that you'll think about how you treat your family. You may feel stressed, but I don't think you want to hurt us because of it. Would you please think about that?"

"All right."

Melanie's mom empathized with Melanie's feelings and tried to give her a vision for going to God with her problems instead of taking it out on the family. As adults, we know that having a positive attitude toward life requires that we trust God instead of focusing on circumstances. It's a specific mind-set that we can help children develop even when they're young.

WHEN ATTITUDES TURN INTO MOODS

A mood is similar to an attitude in some ways, but knowing the differences between it and an attitude will help us know how to respond. Moods tend to last longer, usually have a lower intensity level, and are more global in their reach. A bad mood is a general sense of discontent, hopelessness, anger, depression, or anxiety. An initial problem may have started the negative feeling, but that has long been forgotten, and now everything looks gloomy. You may know how you got into the mood, but even though the event has passed, you can't seem to recover.

An anxious mood is one in which almost any event is considered a potential threat. An angry mood exaggerates irritations and frustrations to be major offenses. In a depressed mood everything feels barren and without meaning. A bad mood is broad in its reach, and everything seems negative. "I don't like this food. There's nothing good on TV. I don't have anything to do. The people around here are irritating. I don't like my room. These clothes are awful." A child stuck in a bad mood seems intent on taking it out on anybody who is nearby.

If not dealt with early, a bad mood can develop into a lifestyle. One mom said, "That's how my seven-year-old son lives every day of his life. It's like living with someone who has continual PMS." We all know adults who have taken on personalities of gloom and doom. It's a sad way to live.

Children stuck in bad moods may need more help to get out. Each person is different, and it's important to understand your child to know which suggestions might work. A child might overcome a bad mood by having a change in routine, getting involved in different activities for a while, or inviting a friend over to play. Some children might overcome a bad mood by serving others and seeing the delight on their faces. Another child may need to go out and rake leaves or sweep the walk instead of just sitting in the bedroom. Some children just need rest or a time of discipline to overcome their selfishness.

Moods can be more of a challenge than attitudes because they don't have a particular issue, problem, or person as a focal point. The key for anyone stuck in a bad mood is to see that life has become self-focused. The solution is to look beyond self. Bad moods have a way of revealing selfishness as a person becomes less concerned about others and lashes out against them.

One mom said, "When my four-year-old daughter gets into one

of her grumpy moods, I take it on as a challenge and try to help her feel better. I hold and rock her, or we just snuggle on the couch. Sometimes we play a tickling game or make cookies together. There are times, however, when nothing I do works and she seems intent on being grumpy. At those times, I say to her, 'There are two kinds of people in the world, happy people and sad people. It looks like you want to be sad for a while, so there's probably not much I can do about it. Let me know when you're feeling better so we can enjoy each other again.' She may have to spend some time alone, but eventually she comes back and things are better." This mom recognized that she could do a number of things to help but ultimately the decision to change was up to her daughter.

Do parents have bad moods? Sure they do. Parents are people too. We all have days we feel depressed, irritable, and frustrated. The goal is to minimize the way you allow your negative feelings to affect how you relate to others. Take time to share with your children what you're feeling. You can teach a lot by modeling how to handle the emotional ups and downs of life.

For children and adults alike, some moods seem to linger longer than others. Sometimes these kinds of moods need intentional work to develop a new kind of thinking. Of course, the real heart change comes from a deepening walk with the Lord. Philippians 2 is a helpful passage in the Bible regarding attitude because it uses Christ as an example. In fact, Philippians 2:3-5 are excellent verses for children to memorize:

> Do nothing out of selfish ambition or vain conceit, but in
> humility consider others better than yourselves. Each of you
> should look not only to your own interests, but also to the
> interests of others. Your attitude should be the same as that
> of Christ Jesus.

Someone stuck in a bad mood often must make a willful decision to change. As parents, our comments can help children think rightly and motivate them to move to a more positive mood. Many people expect feelings to precede actions, but when moving out of a bad mood, actions may need to come first. Encourage your children to pray and then make small positive changes. A smile, a kind word, or a positive action may seem difficult and require faith that God will use those steps to change their feelings. The suggestions you make to your children can help them know how to trust the Lord to get out of negative moods as they get older.

This Is More Complicated Than I Thought

Parents may think that the negative attitudes they see in their child are simply a stage that the child will outgrow. Unfortunately, instead of growing out of bad attitudes, children actually grow into them. If not addressed, these selfish habits will become more entrenched. Getting an attitude tune-up is more than just changing behavior. It means looking inside ourselves and adjusting the way we think and feel.

The Bible says in Romans 12:2 that we can be transformed by the renewing of our mind. Colossians 3:1-2 tells us to set our hearts and our minds on things above. Attitudes are determined by thinking patterns. Education, training, and determination are required to change them. Mere human effort, though, is not enough. God is the one who changes hearts, and attitude adjustment is a walk of faith, learning how to trust God for unseen benefits. As a parent, you can become a strategic influence in your child's life, helping each child understand new ways of thinking and how to choose a more godly attitude.

This isn't easy. You need to become a detective, watching for the bad attitudes, looking for patterns, and solving mysteries. You may need to limit the amount of time your child spends with a friend, increase your child's amount of sleep, decrease television time, or engage more with your child in thoughtful dialogue.

One mom told us about her six-year-old son who came home from school angry almost every day. "When I saw the pattern, I began asking questions. I discovered that he was having a difficult time at school. Learning was hard, and his subjects weren't coming easily to him. He wasn't a discipline problem, and he seemed to do well with his peers, but academics were a challenge. I realized that my son was coming home needing some help from me to unwind. Instead of presenting him with a list of chores or homework to do, I decided to spend some time nurturing and caring for him. I would make him a snack, read him a story, and sometimes just cuddle for a while. This became a special time for us and helped his attitude when he came home."

As a parent, you need to be sensitive to what your children need. Sometimes a comforting hug may help teach them how to receive comfort from God himself. At other times, it's a firm confrontation that will help your children think rightly about life. It's been said, "You can complain because roses have thorns, or you can rejoice because thorns have roses." It's all a matter of perspective. As you patiently work with your children to develop a positive mind-set, you will be giving them a tremendous gift that will last a lifetime.

PUTTING IT ALL TOGETHER

When You See...

A bad attitude in a child, don't overlook or excuse it. Your child may demonstrate attitude problems with an angry tone of voice, gestures, body language, doing an incomplete job, mean words, or by simply withdrawing from others.

Move into a Routine...

Recognize that an attitude has three components and each one is important. The behavior is a flag to see the problem and know *where* to target the change. The emotion helps you know *when* to correct. And the thinking errors show you *what* you need to address.

Because...

Attitudes are windows into a child's heart. If you help your children learn to adjust attitudes, they will have the skills necessary to develop healthy perspectives about life's challenges and struggles as they get older. Children who learn good attitudes when they are young have an easier time relating to God with a good attitude as they grow older.

QUESTIONS FOR FURTHER DISCUSSION

1. Think of a time that your attitude changed toward something because you learned more about it (for example, a sports team, a food, a politician, an organization). What does the connection between right thinking and a good attitude require of parents as they work with their children?

2. Although it may take some time, what are some ways you can help children develop a positive attitude toward eating vegetables, cleaning their rooms, or working hard on homework?

3. What are some difficult or unpleasant things that you've developed a good attitude toward? What do you say to yourself to maintain the good attitude?

DIGGING DEEPER

1. Read Daniel 3:19. Why did the king's attitude change, and how is that similar to the attitude of children sometimes?

2. Read Philippians 2:5. Think about the stories of Christ in the Gospels and list several helpful attitudes that Christ had toward life.

3. Read Romans 12:2. Much of the talk about a positive attitude in our culture comes from a humanistic perspective suggesting that people can achieve great things if they just have a winning attitude. What is the difference between a good attitude that has humanistic roots and one that is based in godliness?

4. Read Ephesians 4:22-24. Using the idea of "put off" and "put on," what are some new attitudes you'd like to see your family develop?

BRINGING IT HOME

Collect several kinds of thermometers from the kitchen, bathroom, garage, and outdoors, along with any devices that have thermostats. Have a discussion with your children about the difference between a thermometer and a thermostat. One is controlled by its environment, and the other sets the temperature. Discuss the following questions:

1. How can you as a child or parent set the emotional temperature of a room when you enter it?

2. When the atmosphere in a family is cloudy or stormy, what can you do to bring pleasant weather into the situation?

3. Do you tend to bring positive or negative weather into family life?

4. How can you be more like a thermostat than a thermometer?

7

Each of you should look not only to your own interests,
but also to the interests of others.

PHILIPPIANS 2:4

"They're So Annoying"

Restraint:
Giving the Gift of Self-Control

Dear Scott and Joanne,

My son, Gregory, can be so annoying. Sometimes I cringe when I see him coming. I know that sounds terrible, but when he gets irritating it's hard for me to be with him. If he's not tapping, or burping, or making some other kind of noise, he's talking and talking and talking, or just bouncing around the house. He's not defiant, and when I tell him to stop, he does, but it only lasts five minutes and he's bothering me again.

Last year, my husband and I decided to try something new. Using the ideas you talk about, we developed a plan. We see that he needs to become more aware of himself and his surroundings and to have the self-control necessary to manage his behaviors.

Now we view the whole problem differently. Instead of getting angry and yelling, we focus on a plan. As soon as he starts in, we move into a routine to help Gregory develop sensitivity and self-control. You wouldn't believe how much this has helped us as a family. When Gregory starts annoying behaviors, I feel like I'm more tolerant and not as angry with him as I used to be. I now have a plan that will train him to be more self-disciplined. I'm surprised at the positive effect this has had on me, too, as I work with him. Thank you.

—Trisha from Wellesley, Massachusetts

Do any of these behaviors sound familiar: bursts of loud noise, tapping, kicking, endless questions, mouth-sounds like heavy breathing, clicking, sirens, burping, grunting, or shrieking? Or what about continual interruptions to conversations or to jobs you're trying to get done?

Some children seem born with an ability to pick up on basic social cues: when to quit, when to be quiet, and when to leave someone alone. Most kids, however, seeming oblivious to the feelings of others, continue to pester, speak without thinking, and be overly silly by pushing, grabbing, teasing, and joking.

If your child has already come to mind, this chapter is for you. It's here that you'll learn to deal with your own emotions as you teach your kids to grow in self-control and sensitivity to others.

Dealing with annoying behavior is not like disciplining for defiance or teaching a child to follow instructions. When it comes to impulsivity, the child can't always make changes just by choosing something different. In many cases, kids don't realize they're being annoying and don't know what's more appropriate. Furthermore, these patterns often come from habits that have been practiced for a long time. These reasons are not excuses for inappropriate behavior, but they're further indications that the job will take concentrated effort from both parents and children.

In many ways, dealing with annoying behaviors is one of the most difficult problems addressed in this book. Part of the issue is immaturity; the child hasn't learned how to pick up on the social cues or restrain behavior as much as we'd like. But these children need more than just time to grow up. They need concentrated work to develop character.

SELF-CONTROL AND SENSITIVITY

Kids who have a problem with annoying behavior need two character qualities: self-control and sensitivity. These qualities not only help children when they are young, but they also become tools for success as they get older.

What Is Self-Control?

The preschooler who whines, the seven-year-old who talks incessantly, the ten-year-old who verbally jabs his brother, and the fourteen-year-old who can't get out of bed in the morning all have one thing in common. They lack self-control. Self-control is the ability to limit behavior rather than give in to present desires. It means you consider a later benefit more important than your present impulse.

Self-control is an important character quality for anyone, adult or child. Most of us wish we could have more of it in our lives. Whether you're trying to have a daily quiet time, exercise regularly, or cut down on caffeine, self-control becomes a determining factor in your success. Self-control helps a person say no to temptation and choose the right course of behavior in difficult situations. It helps people take a stand for righteousness instead of getting sucked into doing something they shouldn't do. Proverbs 25:28 describes it well: "Like a city whose walls are broken down is a man who lacks self-control." Self-control enables people to organize themselves and others, think before they act, save money and time, and make right choices even when unwise opportunities look attractive.

One dad explained self-control to his son this way: "It's irritating when you interrupt me while I'm talking. It's as if you poke me with your finger over and over again. I love you and I try to overlook it, but I'm starting to get bruised. When you have self-control, you will give up the desire to just talk whenever you want so that instead you can love me and care for our relationship. That's what self-control means: choosing to stop yourself and be more sensitive to others."

Some children are gifted with self-control and a host of other organizational skills. Others are more free-spirited, spontaneous, and easygoing; self-control is foreign to them. It's important to take your child's personality into account, but being creative isn't an excuse for irritating others. Character and personality are two different things. Personality provides those unique traits that make a person special

---

Verses About Self-Control to Use with Children

- Like a city whose walls are broken down is a man who lacks self-control. (Proverbs 25:28)
- A fool gives full vent to his anger, but a wise man keeps himself under control. (Proverbs 29:11)
- So then, let us not be like others, who are asleep, but let us be alert and self-controlled. (1 Thessalonians 5:6)
- Encourage the young men to be self-controlled. (Titus 2:6)
- Be self-controlled and alert. Your enemy the devil prowls around like a roaring lion looking for someone to devour. (1 Peter 5:8)

and different. Character adds restraint and richness to a person's life and gives beauty to personality. Character provides your child's personality with the tools necessary to be successful.

What Is Sensitivity?

Children who exhibit annoying behavior also often lack the sensitivity that seems to come naturally to others. Sensitivity is an awareness of one's self and surroundings. A person who is sensitive can pick up on facial expressions or tell that a friend is upset by the way she is walking. Sensitivity helps people see trouble before it gets out of hand so they can take action to prevent greater problems.

Children need sensitivity not only to check their own actions but also to discern when someone else is hurting or needs care. Sensitivity helps kids ask themselves the question, "How is my behavior affecting other people?" Or, "How is the other person feeling, and what can I do to help?"

Some children are overly sensitive. They are very tuned in to the cues around them and sometimes exaggerate their meaning. These children have a tremendous gift but may need to tone down the way they interpret cues. Dustin may cry whenever Mom looks at him a certain way. Krista may interpret her friends' giggling as people laughing at her. These kids are misusing the good character quality of sensitivity and need help understanding how to use it appropriately.

Unfortunately, some children are at the other end of the continuum. These kids can't hear a whispered cue; they need a loud voice. Parents feel embarrassed because their kids require correction at times when the offense seems glaringly obvious. A parent might say, "She should know better by now" or "I shouldn't have to say it so many times." Yes, that's true, but for one reason or another some kids just don't get it. One dad said, "I look at my brother's well-mannered and gracious kids. They wait before interrupting, and when they sense someone is irritated with them, they make changes. My son, on the other hand, doesn't seem to have a clue. I can't understand why he doesn't see it. It's as if he missed out on one of the receiving lines during creation and now he can't seem to function without irritating others."

The good news is that sensitivity can be learned and that you will likely have many opportunities to teach it. As one mom told us, "I was trying to explain sensitivity to my six-year-old son who is continually wild around the house. He'll just run in and make siren noises, or blurt out a question without considering what's already going on in the room. Using the picture of an open door allowing a cold, snowy wind to blow right into the kitchen, I told him, 'That's how I feel when you burst into the room without thinking about me or what

---

Verses About Sensitivity to Use with Children

- Rejoice with those who rejoice; mourn with those who mourn. (Romans 12:15)
- Love is patient, love is kind. (1 Corinthians 13:4)
- Do not let any unwholesome talk come out of your mouths, but only what is helpful for building others up according to their needs, that it may benefit those who listen. (Ephesians 4:29)
- Each of you should look not only to your own interests, but also to the interests of others. (Philippians 2:4)
- Encourage one another and build each other up. (1 Thessalonians 5:11)

I'm doing. I'd like you to try again and come in like sunshine.' He thought that was funny, but it connected. Each time he blasts into the room without sensitivity, I shudder and say, 'Burrrr.' Finally, he's getting the message."

Another mom tried to help her son who got up early in the morning and made a lot of noise. She shared Proverbs 27:14 with him, "If a man loudly blesses his neighbor early in the morning, it will be taken as a curse," and then explained that sensitivity means that we consider how our actions affect others. Once you have a plan, you'll be able to help your children develop the needed character to not only be aware of their own feelings and actions but to be sensitive to others as well.

HELP CHILDREN BY BUILDING THE FENCE

Children who have a problem with annoying behavior need heavier doses of parental control. When you help a child settle down, or encourage another to pick up after himself, you are exerting control. Of course, the goal is self-control, but when a child lacks that valuable quality, parents must step in and provide the parent-control necessary to bridge the gap. In most cases, young children need a lot of parent-control. As they grow older, they take over the "control" job. Parents control less as children begin to demonstrate self-control. Clearly, some kids need more help than others to make this transition.

How can you parent your children in a way that will encourage self-control and sensitivity? Some parents continually remind, even nag, their children. Their approach encourages a dependency on Mom or Dad for neatness, calmness, kindness, and a host of other character qualities. Whose job is it to get homework done, yours or your child's? The way you answer this question will show whether you foster parent-control or self-control in your child. As parents, our goal is to increase our children's ability to monitor and manage their own lives. We prepare the way, but we want our kids to take over the job. We want them to learn to make wise choices and govern their own behavior.

Through limit setting, discipline, and teaching, you provide "fences" that your children need. A fence is an indication of a boundary that shouldn't be crossed. A fence around your house tells neighbors where the limits are and helps children and animals know where their freedom ends. The same is true in social relationships with kids. Children need to know where the social boundaries are and when to stop before behavior becomes a nuisance to others. Children who do annoying things habitually jump the fences. It's as if they walk onto the neighbor's property, step in the flower gardens, and knock over the patio furniture. It's no wonder others get frustrated and angry with them!

Children who have a problem with annoying behaviors need parents who are very involved in their everyday lives. The fences that facilitate social relationships can be complicated at times. An acceptable way to interrupt a friend or sibling is often quite different from how a child may interrupt a teacher at school or a leader at church. Teasing has limits, and knowing when silliness and goofiness should end isn't always easy to determine. Parents must step in at these times to help their children develop the social fences needed for successful relationships.

One dad told us, "It's so frustrating. My son doesn't seem to be able to eat a meal or walk to the car without creating some kind of a conflict. I'm afraid to even leave the room because I know he'll start a problem." This boy needs tighter limits and more supervision. Other children may learn how to respond properly at home but totally lose it when out with others. Teachers and other leaders may report problems they are having with your child that you don't experience. Wherever the problem manifests itself, you need new and creative solutions to help children maintain the fences that are necessary for healthy social interaction.

The goal of parent-control is to encourage self-control. Don't be afraid to provide firm limits for your children. They need those external controls for a while in order to develop internal discipline. After children have learned to live within the boundaries and guidelines you've established for relationships, you gradually release the fences and allow your kids to rely on their own internal fences that they've developed as a result of your training. The work you do during this time has long-lasting benefits. By focusing on impulsivity you will not only help your children socially, but you will also give them the tools to deal with temptation as they get older.

DEVELOP A PLAN

It's important to remember that we're not talking about deliberate defiance in this chapter. Most of the time, children don't mean to annoy or anger their parents in these ways. It's often hard to convince parents of this truth; some parents believe their children are deliberately torturing them. These parents resort to harshness or stronger and stronger consequences in order to force their children to change. This approach makes children feel bad but does little to help them move in a positive direction. We find that impulsiveness and a general lack of awareness of social cues indicate a character weakness that parents must address.

How can you tell the difference between defiance and impulsivity? Sometimes the line is fuzzy, but the biggest factor has to do with awareness. The child exhibiting annoying behavior is often not aware of what he's doing or doesn't have a good repertoire of socially appropriate behaviors. Children do annoying things for at least three reasons: Some children seek attention, and annoying behavior certainly gets them what they want. Other children have nervous habits like twirling hair, tapping, or making various noises with their mouths. Still others are trying to engage in relationships but lack the social cues necessary to be successful.

Whatever the reason, you need a plan to help your child grow in self-control and sensitivity. We have identified four fence posts to help you build and encourage the boundary fences your child needs. As you use these fence posts, you will help your child develop the internal fences needed for success in these areas of life. When you feel your anger rising, use it as a flag, not a solution. Anger can tell you that it's time to pull out the routine you use when annoying behaviors surface.

FENCE POST 1: RAISE THE AWARENESS LEVEL

Many times parents don't have a clear picture of the problem at hand. They're just annoyed. It's important to use the feeling of annoyance to indicate that this is the time to figure out what's going on. Sometimes parents need to become more aware of the problem themselves before they can help their kids see it.

One way to understand the situation is to journal about your child's annoying behavior for a while. Be specific about what annoys you. Breaking the problem into manageable pieces will allow you to be more objective with your kids. Have as much information as possible about the problem before you launch into action.

For example, you probably get frustrated whenever your child begins some annoying behavior. Instead of reacting with harshness, use the emotion as a cue to open your journal and write down details about the situation. When does the problem happen? Are there times when your irritation is worse than others? Where do these annoying behaviors pop up? Out in public? At the dinner table? Try to be as specific as possible. When you can't grab your journal right away, make a quick note to journal later. The more detailed you can get with your observations, the more specific you can be with your plan. Soon, patterns of behavior will jump off the page, and you'll see more clearly what needs to happen next.

Gently Point It Out

After you raise the awareness level for yourself, raise your child's level of awareness. Spend time gently pointing out the problem every time you see it: "Kevin, that's the self-control issue I was talking about." Or, "Kevin, we're getting into that problem again here." Your goal is to help your child see what you're talking about.

One way to raise the awareness level is to develop a silent signal such as a raised finger, a touch on the shoulder, or a raised eyebrow that indicates your child is in one of those situations again. Agree on the signal with your child in advance. Having this kind of discussion communicates that you want to have a coaching relationship with your child. If the child is responsive and wants to change, these nonverbal signals will be helpful. Sometimes, this stage is all that's needed. Soon, Kevin will be saying to himself, "I'm getting into this danger area," and he'll take corrective action himself.

If, on the other hand, your child doesn't respond positively, the child may need to take a break to settle down before you can continue. In this way, you move from a subtle cue like a raised finger to one that is very obvious, like having the child sit in the hall. This progression of cues teaches children that if they can respond to a gentle message, bigger steps will not be taken. After all, that's what it means to be sensitive in social situations. The sensitive person stops talking because she recognizes when someone is getting bored with the conversation. The sensitive employee knows when to back off of the dialogue before he has pushed the boss too far. By using a silent signal you are helping children learn to respond to nonverbal cues, making them more sensitive to the subtle signals in relationships.

Another way you can raise the awareness level is what we call the "observe and run" technique. You don't need a major confrontation every time your child makes a mistake. Sometimes it's the gentle observations that help a child see a negative pattern. Using the observe and run technique, a parent makes a comment and goes about business as usual, not waiting or even asking for a response. "That was the silliness I've been talking about." Or, "You might want to think about the noise you're making with your mouth." Or even, "Do you see what effect your continual tapping is having on your sister?" A child may respond, but you don't have to engage in arguments or even conversation unless you believe it will be productive. Continuing to go about your work leaves the impression that your observation was enough. (Children think about the observations you make much longer than you imagine!)

This "observe and run" technique can be especially helpful as you begin to address new behaviors that need to change. Raising your child's awareness should be done gently, with a coaching attitude. This gives a child time to see the problem without having to deal with the consequences.

Annoyance or Defiance?

During the first few days or week of this plan, don't come on strong with consequences. That may be counterproductive. You wouldn't punish a child who can't remember his math facts or isn't able to tie his shoe. Why? Because the child doesn't need punishment, he needs training. In a similar way, heaping bigger consequences on children for annoying behavior often leads to discouragement and feelings of inadequacy and guilt.

One dad told us, "I used to punish my son for interrupting, thinking that if he kept doing the wrong thing he needed a bigger consequence. He seemed so remorseful, apologizing and committing to change, but in just a few minutes he'd do it again. Instead of teaching my son how to interrupt me graciously, I was pushing him away. He just stopped talking to me altogether. I knew I needed to do something different. My harsh approach wasn't working."

Some parents believe that because they said "stop arguing" yesterday, today's arguing must be defiance. This may not be the case. One mom said, "It took me awhile to realize my son's wildness wasn't always defiance. The problem became clearer to me when I saw him crying after I disciplined him. It wasn't the normal cry, so I asked him why he was upset. He said, 'I don't know what's wrong with me. I want to do the right thing, but I keep forgetting.' I realized that my interpretation of his behavior was too simple. There was more going on here than I realized. As I focused on retraining, I began to see some real improvement, and my son developed hope that he could actually change."

Remember, intentional disobedience and defiance need to be handled differently than annoying behaviors. The child who continues to argue after a parent tells him to stop has entered a different arena and needs work on handling correction. (We discuss that in chapter 4.) Annoying behaviors, by contrast, are best met with a retraining goal in mind.

Change Takes Time

Even after you become aware of a problem, it may take patience to reach a solution. When talking to children about the challenges of making changes in life, I (Scott) like to tell them the story of my softball career. Several years ago I played first base for our church softball team for two seasons. Early in the first season, when I made an out at first base, I'd naturally throw the ball back to the pitcher. One day the coach said, "Hey, Turansky, when you get the guy out, throw the ball around." That made sense to me. I had seen other teams do the same thing after an out, so I determined to make the change. Unfortunately, there weren't any more opportunities in that inning, so by the time I had another chance to practice my new behavior, I had forgotten. So without thinking, I just threw the ball back to the pitcher. The coach yelled with a smile, "Hey, Turansky, throw the ball around."

I immediately knew that I had made a mistake, so I said, "Oh yeah, I'm sorry. Next time." Well the next time came and I was so excited to have gotten the out that I threw the ball back to the pitcher, but after doing so, I realized that I had made a mistake. Before the coach could correct me, I said, "Oops, sorry, Coach. I'll throw it around next time."

Well, it wasn't long before I got another opportunity to work on my new behavior. I still remember that moment. I made the out and started to throw the ball to the pitcher. Before I completed my throw, though, I stopped myself. I paused in midair, turned, and threw the ball to the second baseman. It had taken awhile, but I successfully made a change in my behavior. There's no doubt that I wanted to make the change, but before I could be successful, I had to raise the awareness level of the problem so that I was thinking about what I was doing.

The same thing is true with our children. In order for them to make a significant change, they need to be aware of what the problem is. They need to see it happening. We, as parents, become coaches to our children, providing them with regular feedback to increase their awareness level. Your attitude is very important, and your consistency will help you and your child win in the end.

When God motivates us to change, he first raises our awareness level. We call it conviction. In John 16:8, Jesus said that when he left earth, he would send the Holy Spirit to "convict the world...in regard to sin and righteousness and judgment." The conviction of God enables people to see their need to change. As you raise the awareness level for your children, they become more sensitive to their own actions and to their surroundings. When children grow in sensitivity, they also develop the ability to hear the conviction of the Holy Spirit in their lives. The work you do with your kids now has significant ramifications for their spiritual development.

FENCE POST 2: KEEP CHARACTER IN MIND

When you correct children for annoying behaviors, keep character in mind. In fact, look for other areas in life where you can help your children develop self-control and sensitivity. This will help them handle annoying behaviors with more confidence. Here are some things you can do to teach self-control and sensitivity in proactive ways.

Offer Alternatives

Many parents only use negative techniques to deal with annoying behavior. It's not enough, however, to teach children what they *shouldn't* be doing. "Stop tapping," "Quit pestering," or "Don't interrupt" are not enough for real training to take place. Children need to know what they should do instead. You might say, "Molly, your humming is distracting your brother from his homework. Please be more sensitive and go into the other room if you want to hum."

"Sasha, your continual talking is making me tired. Let's just be quiet for a while."

"Tom, you need to stop. Your interruptions are unkind. You can say 'excuse me' and show your self-control by waiting."

Your response shouldn't tell children only what's wrong, but should also teach them what's appropriate.

Define Your Words

Another key to teaching proactively is to define your terms in a way that your child can understand. We aren't suggesting a dictionary definition, but rather a working definition that can help your child on a daily basis. In fact, the definition may be different for each child because character works itself out differently depending on your child's personality and habits. Here are some definitions to get you started.

Self-control is the ability to control myself so that Mom and Dad don't have to.

Self-control means to think before I act.

Self-control is the ability to talk about problems instead of grabbing, pushing, or hitting.

Self-control means that I limit the noises I make when others are around.

Self-control means that I focus on one thing until it gets done before I move to the next.

Sensitivity means that when I walk into a room I look and listen before I speak.

Sensitivity is thinking about how my actions are affecting other people.

Sensitivity means thinking about how I could help someone else.

These working definitions are helpful because they tie character to behavior in practical ways. Instead of vague principles, you're giving kids hands-on ways to live out these character qualities.

In order to develop an effective definition for your child, you need to first identify an area where your child struggles. Next ask yourself, What is it that I want my child to do differently? Finally, think about how the character quality of self-control or sensitivity fits into this picture. Put it all together in some kind of definition and start using it. When your daughter needs correction, have her repeat the definition. Repeating it over and over will help build right thinking patterns.

Choose Your Consequences Carefully

One of the differences between punishment and discipline is the motive. Punishment is a sentence for a crime committed. Discipline is a teaching and learning experience. When parents get fed up with a behavior, they often sentence a child to her room, take away a privilege, or give a heavy dose of angry words. Instead, look for consequences that teach or ones that build the internal awareness level or increase the self-control skills. A child might need to sit quietly for five minutes just for the practice, or leave the room for a few minutes and come back with a plan for another course of action next time. Here are some other positive suggestions parents might make:

"Okay, instead of my responding in anger right now, let's stop our normal pattern. I'd like you to think about several warning signs that show we were entering the same problem again. Let's look for the cues so that we can change earlier." Or...

"How would you like me to correct you in these moments? What you're doing is not good, and I need some way to help you see it so that you can make changes." Or...

"Here's a Bible verse about self-control. Please make it
into a card to put up somewhere so that you'll see it every
day." Or...

"You need to take a minute and write a letter describing the
problem and your plan for making changes."

Seek Out Mentors for Your Child

Another way to help your child's character development is to recruit
other mentors to teach it. All parents should be grateful for the youth
workers, teachers, counselors, and activity leaders who say the same
things that parents try to say to their children. It always surprises me
(Joanne) when one of my children comes home from some kind of
activity with a challenge from a leader or a new way of looking at life.
Sometimes I feel like saying, "I've been telling you that for years," but
instead I simply smile and say, "Oh, what a wise youth leader you have."

As children get older, it may be helpful for them to get a job outside the home. Although this adds other issues to the parent/child
relationship, a job can be a good way for your child to learn self-control. Regular accountability from a manager or boss instills character.
Volunteering with a community service organization or local business
can have many of the same benefits by giving a child the opportunity
to serve others while working under the authority of another adult.

Children learn self-control by memorizing scripture, playing an
instrument, and getting involved in sports, drama, and other
extracurricular activities. The most important thing is not the activity; it's the teacher who places an emphasis on developing character.

Model Sensitivity

Working on sensitivity requires listening with more than just ears.
Talk to children about how to listen and how to pick up cues from a

situation. My (Scott) wife, Carrie, has taught me a lot about sensitivity. When we were fixing up our first home, we were continually looking for new ideas. Often we would leave a friend's house and Carrie would say, "Did you see the pattern in their carpet? I like that." I would respond with, "What carpet?" In another home she would say, "I liked their wallpaper." I never saw it. After a while, though, when I went into a home, I would take time to look at the details so that Carrie and I could talk about them afterwards. I developed sensitivity to my surroundings as I practiced making observations each time I went into someone's home.

Children need the same kind of training. "Did you see how the cashier looked flustered?" "Grandma sure seemed happy today." "I liked the smile on your brother's face when you came into the room. He seemed eager to see you." Your observations about the emotional atmosphere in a situation can help your children begin to see it for themselves.

Informal discussions and telling and reading stories can also encourage self-control and sensitivity. One mom said, "As I read the newspaper or listen to the radio I'm on the lookout for ways I can illustrate the importance of self-control and sensitivity in life. This week I told the story to my children about our mayor who offended a group of people because he spoke without thinking. I've also talked with them about road rage and how people get carried away and hurt others when they don't have self-control. These stories make the things I'm trying to teach seem more real to my children."

FENCE POST 3: PRAISE IN THE PROCESS

The third fence post that builds and encourages internal boundaries in children is parents' praise. Many parents tend to focus on the mistakes their kids make—and when a child has a problem with impulsivity, there sure are a lot! If you're going to help a child change, learn to affirm approximately right behavior. Parents sometimes save their praise until their child gets it perfect. Unfortunately, children can become discouraged before they get there. You can do a lot to encourage your kids by praising them in the process.

Children need praise, so when you observe small steps of progress, indulge them with affirmation. In doing so, you'll bring hope to your kids and help them see the light at the end of the tunnel. This will help keep them moving in the right direction. Look for things that your children are doing well. Point those things out. Identify landmarks of progress and share those with your kids.

Many kids need step-by-step instructions for handling simple tasks in life, such as seeing someone's annoyance or walking into a room quietly to sense the situation before talking. Break your instructions down into smaller pieces so that you'll have many opportunities to offer praise for progress. Each piece becomes a step that clarifies in practical terms what your child needs to be working on. Changing big patterns is tough, but smaller steps of change seem more manageable and help a child achieve the success you desire.

One mom said, "My son, Taylor, had a problem being silly when it wasn't appropriate. His silliness irritated the family. His dad and I began to work with him by dividing the problem into three parts. The first had to do with timing. We agreed that Taylor is funny and we all enjoy his ability to bring humor into our family, but we asked him to evaluate if now was the best time. Next, we asked him to think about whether the kind of silliness was appropriate for the situation. And third, we asked him to pay attention to when it was time to stop. Whenever we were feeling annoyed by Taylor's silliness, we would just use a word or phrase as a reminder to help him know which of the three was a problem: 'Timing,' 'Appropriate,' 'Time to stop.' As we began to see improvement, or even accidental right choices, we praised him. Taylor began to learn how to guide his humor in the right direction."

It can be hard to praise children who have habits of annoying behavior. After all, the absence of irritation for a few moments doesn't usually release an overwhelmingly positive feeling. You may even feel fearful that the inevitable will return at any moment, and you're just resting up for the next battle. Remember that life offers good character building curriculum, and you are part of the process. Take extra time, if necessary, to help your kids catch a vision for maturity. Concentrate on ways to lead them to success. Praise can go a long way.

There are some things you can teach when things are going well that you can't teach when things are going poorly. Don't miss those opportunities. Children need to know what "doing well" looks like, how it feels to succeed, and the encouragement they get from pleasing God and their parents. When children are doing well, you want them to enjoy it so they'll want to stay there instead of migrating to behavior that is unproductive. Your response to your children in those moments becomes the motivation to keep them on the right track.

FENCE POST 4: DEVELOP TOLERANCE

One mom said, "One of the advantages of having children is that I have become much more tolerant of loud noises." Well, we don't believe tolerance is the whole answer, but it sure helps you choose your battles instead of reacting without warning.

Tolerance is the distance an action must go before it sets off a reaction in you. We're not suggesting that you just let things go and forget about them. Rather, you need to have a measured response instead of a short fuse. Parents who quickly react with harshness to a child's impulsivity lose opportunities to teach. Instead, they contribute to patterns of emotional intensity that weaken the relationship and damage the learning process.

Some days, when it seems like everything your son does is irritating, you feel like a police officer, blowing the whistle each time he gets out of line. In those moments it's often helpful to rank the offenses

---

When you don't know whether to address your child's annoying behavior in a particular situation, ask yourself:

- Can I comment on this behavior without being rude or harsh?
- Is this behavior part of something I'm working on with my child?
- Is this behavior just annoying me because of my current mood?
- Would my comments help my child build the character qualities he/she is lacking right now?
- Would my tone reflect how much I value our relationship?
- Would it be better to let things go this time because...
    - I'm working on other problems with my child at the moment?
    - I've already corrected too much today?
    - the atmosphere in our relationship right now needs more affirmation than correction?
    - my child is feeling discouraged?
    - we are in too public a situation?
    - I don't feel I would have enough self-control myself right now to handle my words in a loving way?

---

from 1 to 3, 1 being the worst and needing the most intervention and 3 being negative behaviors you could live with for a while. Focus on the 1s and let the others go for now. This will prevent your relationship with your child from becoming a constant battleground. Of course, this means you let things go that you might not otherwise tolerate, but as you begin to see change, you can address those other tolerated behaviors as well. The wise parent knows that change takes time and winning a battle isn't as important as winning a relationship.

When you must discipline for the same thing over and over again, it's helpful to view yourself as a "reality wall" that the child keeps running into in an attempt to find direction. That wall has to be unemotional and controlled, not easily irritated, but at the same time something that provides a firm boundary. You want your child to learn to head in the right direction because of godly character, not because of fear of an explosive parent. One mom said, "The wall illustration has helped me a lot. I used to become more intense when my daughter needed repeated correction. Now instead of becoming more harsh, I simply continue with the correction, and my firmness helps bring about change. I just have to hang in there and be a wall."

If you don't react each time you see a problem, you can also more carefully analyze the problem itself. Why is this happening? What is she thinking? When does this happen the most? What do we want her to do instead? Moving into an analytical mode instead of an emotional one can be more effective.

The Importance of Prayer

The greatest source of strength in these moments of frustration for parents is prayer. Because Donny had been annoying, Mom sent him to his room. After a while he emerged and informed his mother that he had thought it over and said a prayer.

"That's good," Mom replied. "If you ask God to help you not be annoying, he will."

"Oh, I didn't ask him to help me not be annoying. I asked him to help you put up with me."

Prayer does many things. It calls on God to bring about change. It enables the power of the Holy Spirit to work in both the parent and child in the midst of the process. And prayer changes the hearts of those who pray. If you regularly pray for your son and his annoying behaviors or your daughter and her irritating habits, you will find yourself being a more gracious coach, partnering with the Lord to encourage the necessary changes. You're just a tool used in the Master's hands—not a passive tool, but one that is actively working, learning, and developing new strategies and approaches. As you rely on God and ask him for help, you will see marked improvement, not just in your child's behavior, but also in the way that you interact. Regular prayer is worth the investment. One dad set his watch to beep on the hour just to remind him to pray for his son. It was a continual reminder of God's work in the life of his family.

The Need for Forgiveness

Dealing with annoying behavior in children requires a tremendous amount of patience and forgiveness. Children make mistakes and often don't respond well to correction. Parents try to be firm and look for creative ways to teach, raise awareness, and encourage sensitivity and self-control. In most cases, change comes slowly. It's at these times that forgiveness is needed in very practical terms. Peter asked Jesus how many times he needed to forgive. Seven times? Peter thought he was way over the reasonable limit. (Of course, he didn't try to raise some of the children we're working with!) Jesus' answer was a rebuke: "I tell you, not seven times, but seventy-seven times" (Matthew 18:22).

Many parents have exceeded that number with their children long ago. The point, however, that Jesus was making doesn't have to do with a number. In essence, Jesus was saying, "You need to have a lifestyle of forgiveness."

Forgiving children doesn't mean we ignore offenses. Rather, forgiveness opens the door for significant confrontation to take place. Instead of taking the offense personally, you release the emotional intensity so that you can help a child develop character. The fact of the matter is that most kids don't appreciate the correction and amazing patience we have as parents. But the lack of gratefulness we receive in this job of parenting doesn't lessen our task. We must continually correct our kids while looking for ways to do it that they can accept. Plan your comments and present the critique in constructive and gracious ways. Forgiveness frees you from harshness and allows for controlled, consistent training to take place. Tolerance is easier when you don't have accumulated frustration. Forgiveness allows you to release offenses instead of saving them up.

WHAT ABOUT MY OTHER KIDS?

When a family has a child who struggles with annoying behavior, it affects the whole family. It's important to consider each child's needs. A child who does annoying things may attract more attention from Mom or Dad. These children may need more one-on-one time than the others. Be sure to give the necessary attention to other children as well. That doesn't mean that you even things out or try to give equal attention to all. The most important thing is that you consider each child's needs and respond to each one accordingly. After all, God, our Heavenly Father, doesn't treat all his children the same. He gives out talents in differing amounts and spiritual gifts that are uniquely designed for each of us. In the same way, teach character to your kids according to their uniqueness, and help them develop the qualities they need to be successful.

Annoying behaviors irritate siblings and can lead to tense relationships. Your other children might easily explode when annoying behaviors persist. Take time to help your other children learn to deal with irritation. One mom said, "I empathize with Nicholas when he gets frustrated with Allie's behavior. I want him to know that what Allie's doing is wrong. It's annoying and I'm working on helping her change. But Nicholas doesn't think I'm doing enough. He thinks I should be stricter. I have to admit that sometimes Nicholas is right. I explain to him that I've never raised an Allie before. I even explain some of my strategy ideas to Nicholas to help him appreciate what I'm trying to do. He seems to be more understanding. Lately, I've seen him trying to do some of the same things with his sister that I'm doing. It's not easy, and Nicholas still gets frustrated, but I feel like he and I are partners in dealing with his response to Allie, just as I feel like Allie and I are partners in working on annoying behaviors. It's done a lot to maintain our relationships as we work on this problem."

Developing tolerance, giving gracious feedback, prayer, and parental guidance can help a child learn to relate to a brother or sister who has annoying behaviors. In the process, children will learn skills for dealing with people that will equip them for the rest of their lives. After all, there are a lot of annoying adults. Children who learn how to relate to siblings in healthy ways often do better relating to other people as they get older.

I FEEL EXASPERATED AND WANT TO GIVE UP

Last year my (Joanne) neighbor planted a young tree in his front yard. He tied four ropes as supports from the trunk to the ground. The ropes provided the stability as the tree grew that first year. The ropes were inconvenient to walk around and didn't look all that attractive, so this year he removed them. The tree is continuing to grow and now has the internal strength to stand on its own without falling. Children who lack self-control and sensitivity are like that young tree, needing support and control for a period of time. Parenting these children requires extra work and is often inconvenient, but it's worth it in the end.

Don't simply endure your kid's weaknesses or assume that they will outgrow insensitivity and impulsivity. Use the opportunities you have now to help your children develop godly character. Pray for your children regularly, recognizing that self-control is a fruit of the Spirit (Galatians 5:23) and that God is at work in your child's heart. In fact, God uses struggle to develop character (Romans 5:3-4), so be careful that you don't make life too easy for your kids. They need to feel the consequences of their actions, and your gentle coaching will help to build the character they need.

The goal isn't to turn your child into "Miss Manners" overnight (although that would be the dream of many parents). Rather, keep in mind the final aim: developing self-control and sensitivity. Change takes time. Too much pressure can be overwhelming for your child. Patience in you is an important part of the plan. Some parents become angry with their children when they don't see immediate change. One dad observed, "It's interesting that when we bump into someone on the street we say 'excuse me.' When we bump into our child we yell, 'Get out of the way!'"

If you focus on too many areas to change all at once, you and your child may become discouraged. Using the fence posts described in this chapter, choose two or three areas of concern to address first. You may only present one area at a time if that's all your child can handle. Add additional ones as your child makes progress. Remember that you are working for long-term benefits. Your children need self-control and sensitivity to be successful in life. As your children grow, they will experience temptations of many kinds, and you are helping to develop the character to address those temptations in a godly way.

PUTTING IT ALL TOGETHER

When You See...

Annoying behaviors such as interrupting, lack of awareness of others, and socially inappropriate behavior, don't just ignore them. Recognize that you need to work with your children in gentle but firm ways.

Move into a Routine...

To develop character. Become the temporary fence your children need to build their own internal fences. Use the four fence posts:

1. Raise the Awareness Level
2. Keep Character in Mind
3. Praise in the Process
4. Develop Tolerance

Because...

You are helping your children develop self-control and sensitivity. These qualities will help children not only deal with annoying behaviors now but will develop in them the character to handle temptation as they grow older. Instead of responding impulsively, they will have the tools to respond with restraint.

QUESTIONS FOR FURTHER DISCUSSION

1. List a few of your pet peeves. These are things that tend to make you angry, such as discovering the toothpaste left out

or not being able to find your scissors. What do you do in those moments that is helpful or not helpful?

2. Identify an area that you're working on in your life (that is, diet, exercise, anger, time management) that is taking some time to change. How might an understanding of your own change process help you as you work with your children?

3. What are some creative ways to raise the awareness level of an annoying behavior in your family?

DIGGING DEEPER

1. How might Proverbs 12:16 and Ecclesiastes 7:9 help you and your family?

2. How was the character quality of sensitivity useful for Jesus when he addressed a problem in Matthew 26:6-13?

3. Peter demonstrated impulsiveness in Matthew 14:28-30; Matthew 17:1-4; and Matthew 26:51-52. What is the good side of impulsiveness in Peter's life and in the lives of our children?

4. Peter gave in to temptation by denying Christ three times. He later wrote the two epistles in which he speaks of self-control four times (1 Peter 1:13; 4:7; 5:8; and 2 Peter 1:6). What had Peter learned, and what does he want us to understand about self-control?

BRINGING IT HOME

Make a Positive Behavior Journal for each of your children. For young children, this may be a picture book; for an older child or teenager, it may look more like a journal. On the spot or at the end of the day, allow each child to write one of the behaviors you pointed out that was helpful or positive. Be sure to tell them what character quality that behavior demonstrated. You may even cut pictures out of magazines that reflect some aspect of that character quality. Share the book with others, when appropriate, to reinforce the positive character growing in each of your children.

8

The LORD detests lying lips,
but he delights in men who are truthful.

PROVERBS 12:22

"They Lie"

Honesty:
Giving the Gift of Integrity

Dear Scott and Joanne,

I don't know if I was more angry or afraid. My daughter's habitual lying seemed out of control. Although I couldn't prove it, often the things she said just didn't sound right. One time I got a report back from my neighbor, "So I hear you guys are moving to Idaho..." When I confronted my daughter she denied it and made up another story. She wouldn't take responsibility for her lying and just created more lies to cover up the previous ones. I had hoped she'd grow out of it, but things just got worse.

I knew we needed a plan. As you suggested, we started watching her more closely, checking up on her, and trying to confirm her stories. We prayed for her and with her about the subject of honesty, and we've come down pretty hard with the consequences. We've taught her from the Bible and through day-to-day conversations about what honesty is and why it's important.

We now see that dishonesty is a great source of temptation for her in her life. We are determined to work on this diligently, not only for now, but also for our daughter's future well-being and success.

—Janna from Findlay, Ohio

Truth is foundational to relationships. It helps us know and understand others so that we can interact with them effectively. When people are honest and tell the truth, we learn to trust them. When a person lies, our thinking about that person changes. Trust is broken. This is particularly hurtful when it's our children who break our trust. We want to believe our kids. We want to give them the benefit of the doubt. We want to trust them. When a child lies, we're stuck. We ask, "How can she do this to me? Why would he lie to me?" Our very relationship feels threatened.

One mom said, "When I realized that my daughter sometimes lied to me, I began to question all her actions and her answers to my questions. 'What is she trying to get away with now?' I would wonder." This girl had lost a valuable asset: the benefit of the doubt. Now, instead of assuming that she's done a thorough job, Mom checks out small details. Even when her daughter unintentionally forgets something, Mom may perceive it as dishonesty.

Lying is an attack on our closeness with our children. It makes us feel angry and betrayed. But the solution is not to yell, or punish, or demand the truth. Overpowering or forcing specific words will do little to develop integrity in our children. What we need is a plan. We need to understand the deeper problem and get to the heart of our children.

WHAT IS A LIE?

Lying is one form of deception. While almost everyone agrees that lying is wrong in general, even relationship experts disagree about whether lying is acceptable in certain situations. This leaves families with a challenge to know when and how to tell the truth. The subject is surprisingly complicated. In order to deal with lying in children, we first need to define what lying is so that we understand what we're talking about. Families have different standards to determine what's acceptable and what's not.

Take the following Lie Detector Test. Get a piece of paper and write the numbers one to ten. Ask yourself which of the following scenarios would be considered lying in your home. We'll discuss the answers as we go along in this chapter.

Lie Detector Test

1. Mom, hearing a car drive into the driveway, calls to her two children, "Dad's home, please come to the table to eat." After a minute or so, a knock on the door reveals that the car belonged to a friend from church who was stopping by. Amy, age six, turns to Mom and says, "Daddy isn't home. You lied." *Is Mom lying?*

2. Seventeen-year-old Michael arrives home just in time for Mom's birthday dinner. Mom is surprised and with delight says, "Oh, Mike, thank you for getting off work early for my party." Mike replies, "Getting off work wasn't hard. It was canceling my appointment with the president and rescheduling my trip to Rome that was tough—but I took care of it all so I wouldn't miss this event for you, Mom." *Of course, Michael didn't really have to cancel those events. Is Michael lying?*

3. Dad plays with his three-year-old daughter as they look at
    a picture book of different animals. Joy has just figured
    out how to get a fun reaction from Dad, and he, enjoying
    the interaction with his daughter, plays up the game.
    "What's that?" Dad says as he points to the chicken. "It's
    a cow," says Joy. "No, it's a chicken," says Dad playfully as
    they both laugh together. Dad continues by pointing to a
    rabbit, "What's this?" "It's a cow," says Joy, waiting eagerly
    for Dad's playfully shocked response. "No, it's a rabbit,"
    says Dad as they continue to have fun together.
    Is Joy lying?

4. Thirteen-year-old Charissa answers the phone and says,
    "Hi, Pastor Andrews." Mom quietly says, "Tell him I'm
    not home." Charissa turns to her mom and whispers,
    "That's lying. I'm not going to tell him that." Mom
    replies, "Okay, I'll go outside, and then you can tell him
    I'm not home right now." Charissa plays along with Mom's
    plan and tells the pastor, "Mom stepped out for a little
    while," but only after Mom leaves the house. *Is Charissa
    lying?*

5. When fifteen-year-old Morgan arrives late to school, her
    teacher asks her why. "We got held up in traffic," Morgan
    offers. While it is true that there was an unusual amount of
    traffic that morning, Morgan also slept through her alarm,
    getting her and her mom out of the house later than usual.
    Is Morgan lying?

6. Eleven-year-old Jacob has overheard the doctor say that
    Grandma's tests came back pretty bad and that she only has
    a few weeks to live. In the doctor's professional opinion, he
    believes it's best not to tell her everything right now since
    she's so sick. A few minutes later, when Jacob was with

Grandma, she asked him if he knew how her tests came out. Jacob, not knowing how to respond, said, "I don't know." *Is Jacob lying?*

7. In ten-year-old Noah's science class at school, the teacher had the students conduct interviews in the local mall to measure how long people would tolerate a boring questionnaire. Their assignment was to go up to individuals, introduce themselves, invite the person to participate in a survey about clothing styles, and then see at what point in the hundred-question interview the person would decide that he or she had to go. Noah began his interview by saying, "Hi, my school is doing research about clothing styles. Could I ask you a few questions?" *Is Noah lying?*

8. Alison, age nine, could hardly wait to leave the boring party. As she says good-bye to the host, she says, "I enjoyed your party. Thank you very much for inviting me." *Is Alison lying?*

9. Mrs. Simpson stops fifteen-year-olds Rachel and Tammi in the hall during class without a hall pass. Tammi lies and says that they were just on their way to class and were a little late, when in reality they had decided to skip the class altogether. Rachel is silent. *Is Rachel lying?*

10. "I don't know what happened to the computer. The file isn't here," Philip said to his teacher after he accidentally deleted the file. *Is Philip lying?*

The preceding situations pose common ethical dilemmas for children. Each scenario helps us understand a little more about what lying is and what it isn't. It is important to understand specifically what a lie is in order to teach your children about honesty.

THE TRUTH ABOUT LYING

"Deception" is a term we use to describe a number of dishonest words or actions. Lying is only one piece of the bigger puzzle. Some people define lying as saying something that is not true, but we believe lying has more to do with the intent of the speaker. The person who reports inaccurate information is just mistaken unless he intends to deceive. We believe that lying is best defined this way:

Lying is stating something, either written, oral, or with other signals, with the intent to mislead.

In other words, lying has two components: (1) a statement of one kind or another, and (2) the intent to mislead.

First, lying involves *making a statement.* That statement may be in the form of written language, spoken words, or even gestures or other nonverbal cues. The person who points one way when asked where the bad guy is, in order to send the pursuers in the wrong direction, lies by making a statement with actions.

The second component of lying is the *intent to mislead.* This helps us understand why Mom's statement in Situation 1 is not a lie. Although Mom said something that wasn't true—Dad was home— it wasn't a lie because she wasn't intending to deceive. She was just mistaken.

When Michael reports that he cancelled his appointment with the president and his trip to Rome for his mom's party in Situation 2, he wasn't intending to deceive. He expected that his mom would understand the joke and know that he really didn't have those plans. He was exaggerating in fun, and they both knew it. That's not wrong. In the same way, Dad and Joy play a fun game about pictures of animals in Situation 3. Joy and Dad are teasing, and they both understand that. It's not lying because no one is trying to mislead the other. They are just playing a game.

This brings us to an interesting problem. Sometimes when children are caught lying they will say, "I was just joking" or "I didn't

---

Verses That Talk About Lying

- There are six things the LORD hates, seven that are detestable to him: haughty eyes, a lying tongue, hands that shed innocent blood, a heart that devises wicked schemes, feet that are quick to rush into evil, a false witness who pours out lies and a man who stirs up dissension among brothers. (Proverbs 6:16-19)
- Truthful lips endure forever, but a lying tongue lasts only a moment. (Proverbs 12:19)
- The LORD detests lying lips, but he delights in men who are truthful. (Proverbs 12:22)
- Peter said, "Ananias, how is it that Satan has so filled your heart that you have lied to the Holy Spirit and have kept for yourself some of the money you received for the land? Didn't it belong to you before it was sold? And after it was sold, wasn't the money at your disposal? What made you think of doing such a thing? You have not lied to men but to God." (Acts 5:3-4)
- Do not lie to each other, since you have taken off your old self with its practices and have put on the new self, which is being renewed in knowledge in the image of its Creator. (Colossians 3:9-10)

---

really mean it." They know that this would be a viable excuse. Children need to understand that the difference between joking and lying has to do with intent and with whether or not they are believed. We need to be careful when we tease or joke. The other person needs to realize that the words we're saying are just for fun and not go on thinking that what we said is true.

If your son says, "There are no more chocolate chips," to deceive you because he wants to sneak some into his backpack, he's lying. If he says, "There are no more chocolate chips," as a joke because you need another cup for the cookies and he is teasing you, that's okay as long as he's just playing a game. Children need to understand the difference between these two types of scenarios and realize that they can't change their minds about the intent after they say the words.

A Time for Joking

A warning is in order here. In a family where a lot of play includes saying things that are untrue or misleading, family members may be more susceptible to lying in other areas of life. Telling stories that aren't true becomes easier and can make lying easier as well. Also, you may develop a reputation for yourself that says, "You can't always believe me." I (Joanne) know a man who enjoys teasing and joking as a way to make conversation. Often he says things that aren't true, but he begins in a way that's quite convincing. As the story goes on, the joke becomes apparent. This kind of teasing can be funny, but it also carries the risk of developing a negative reputation. It's hard to believe anything this man says. Joking with falsehood can lead some families to the conclusion that this kind of teasing is inappropriate.

The way a family handles the truth is important. Although some teasing may involve misrepresenting the truth and can be an acceptable part of play, it's important to ask some serious questions about where that play is leading. If you're having a problem with lying in your family, you may want to cut out even playful teasing in this area to help children see the issues more clearly.

One mom told us, "We have a problem with lying in our family. As I began developing a plan to deal with it, I noticed that the way we play often encourages deception. If my four-year-old comes into the kitchen to ask, 'What's for dinner?' I might jokingly reply, 'Frog Soup.' Our family fun is not necessarily bad as we play small tricks and tease each other, but I'm seeing now that we need to take a break from those kinds of activities for a while. It may be that our fun is inadvertently encouraging our children to be dishonest."

This mom is wrestling with an important issue. Sometimes the things you do or say aren't bad in and of themselves, but you may need to make adjustments because of the particular needs of your family.

Word Play

Some children believe that they can mislead people by splitting hairs on the definition of words. "I wasn't running, I was walking very fast," may be an excuse a child gives in the hallway at church. The issue here reaches the heart of what communication is and what part words play in the process. Words are vehicles that carry a message from one person to another. The message isn't in the words themselves but in the intent of the person speaking those words. It's important for children who try to play with words in this way to recognize that they're misusing language. Words taken out of context or an individual word by itself may communicate something completely different than the speaker had in mind. The important question to ask is not "What words did the speaker use?" but "What was the speaker's intent?"

One day when my (Joanne) son Tim was about two years old, he went to play in the backyard. As he headed out the door with his brother, I reminded him, "Stay out of the mud." I was only a few minutes behind them, but by the time I got outside, Tim was already muddy. When I questioned him, he replied, "It's just wet dirt." I couldn't help smiling. I knew, though, that what's cute at two years old, if not addressed, can grow into a serious problem of lying as children get older. Kids need to learn to follow the intent of the instruction, and if it's unclear they need to ask questions to clarify your meaning.

In Situation 4, when Charissa told the pastor that Mom "just stepped out," she may have thought she was telling the truth because Mom had stepped out of the house. But those words, although true in themselves, were intended to mislead Pastor Andrews. In normal communication "she stepped out for a while" communicates the idea that Mom has left the home and is inaccessible, not that she stepped out onto the porch to avoid a phone call. By defining words for her own purposes, Charissa misused language and mistakenly believed she was telling the truth. Although technically her words were true, she was misleading Pastor Andrews by redefining those words. Her mother participated in the deception and encouraged her daughter to lie.

Morgan makes a similar mistake in Situation 5. She thinks that if she only tells part of the truth and avoids any false statements, she has not lied. She uses the truth to mislead her teacher. In this situation we see that the simple definition, "lying is saying something that's not true," is inadequate. Sometimes people can lie using part of the truth as a weapon. The point is that sharing only part of the truth, with the intent of misleading someone, can be just as much a lie as saying something totally false.

Little White Lies

In our culture, some lies are considered acceptable and are often called "white lies." These lies aren't considered hurtful and are even thought to provide some benefit. People often try to justify lying in three areas in particular: medical situations, psychological testing, and socially awkward situations. In Situation 6, Grandma is sick and the knowledge that she is dying may cause her to respond poorly or give up hope. Some believe that lying to sick patients is not only acceptable but is actually beneficial. We disagree. Although wisdom may dictate what information is shared with a patient, we don't believe that lying is appropriate at any time. In these difficult situations a person may refuse to answer a question or even postpone a difficult conversation till later. Withholding information without intent to deceive is not lying.

Similarly, some justify lying in cases where surveys and psychological testing require that the questioner mislead people to gain pertinent information as in Noah's science project in Situation 7. Some find this acceptable because of the good gained. Lying undercuts basic tenets of relationships, however, and over the long term hurts those who rely on it. For example, many people have a hard time believing anything that a used car salesman says because used car salesmen have developed a reputation of misleading potential buyers. The same is true of people who conduct surveys. People begin to second-guess them and wonder what's behind every question. Other ways of gathering information are available and can be used to learn about people without resorting to lying.

Some people try to justify lies in awkward social experiences as well. When Alison, in Situation 8, leaves the party, she doesn't want to hurt her friend's feelings, so she lies about enjoying the party. Many people justify these lies because they think the only alternative is a blunt version of the truth that hurts the feelings of others. Those who justify these social lies usually do so by suggesting that they don't do harm but actually make people feel good. Because they think that the alternative is bluntness, and they don't want to hurt someone's feelings, lying becomes an acceptable solution.

Tact is certainly needed in many social situations, but tact doesn't require that you lie. It may be helpful to share an actual compliment or honest statement like "Thank you for inviting me this evening. I had a conversation with Tommy that really got me thinking." If you're having trouble finding something nice to say, maybe you need to work a little harder at it. After all, lying is a shortcut when the truth, for one reason or another, doesn't seem attractive. If social grace requires you to give a compliment as you leave a party, why not consider a genuine one like "You have a nice house for a party" or "Parties are a lot of work. Thank you for pulling it all together." Children may not know how to demonstrate tact or grace in such situations, but parents can use those teachable moments to train their children to be honest and gracious.

In Situation 9, Rachel didn't lie, but her friend did. Rachel's silence, however, makes her guilty because she participated in the

---

Verses That Talk About the Truth

- Stand firm then, with the belt of truth buckled around your waist, with the breastplate of righteousness in place. (Ephesians 6:14)
- Jesus answered, "I am the way and the truth and the life. No one comes to the Father except through me." (John 14:6)
- LORD, who may dwell in your sanctuary? Who may live on your holy hill? He whose walk is blameless and who does what is righteous, who speaks the truth from his heart. (Psalm 15:1-2)
- Kings take pleasure in honest lips; they value a man who speaks the truth. (Proverbs 16:13)

deception. Remaining silent and allowing others to believe something that's false is another form of deception, but it isn't lying. All forms of deception provide teachable opportunities for families. Withholding the truth, coloring a story, exaggerating, pretending, and allowing people to believe something false all provide ethical dilemmas that make for excellent discussions. A person of integrity approaches these problems carefully and looks for solutions that emphasize both truth and love in proper balance.

Why Children Lie

Situation 10 is an illustration of the most common reason children lie: to escape punishment. They fear what might happen if they tell the truth, so they try to protect themselves. Philip chose to lie rather than admit that he accidentally deleted the file. Children sometimes think that lying is the easy way out, but, in fact, it often makes life more difficult. The child who is prone to lie in challenging situations demonstrates poor character. If not dealt with, deceit gets worse.

Avoiding punishment isn't the only reason children lie. Some children lie to get ahead or appear better than they really are. The stress on individualism and competition in our society along with the goal of achieving material success generate intense pressure to cut corners for adults as well as children. Deceit can reap great rewards. Our society even accepts a certain amount of dishonesty. An adult may be expected to exaggerate skills and experience on a job application or paint a better-than-reality picture of a student on a college reference letter. The temptation, of course, is to develop a lifestyle of deception that makes oneself appear better than one really is. It's a dangerous path but one that is very tempting for both children and adults.

When children don't like something about themselves and would rather be someone different, they sometimes cover up their perceived faults with a veil of dishonesty. In the end they are saying, "If you knew who I really am you wouldn't like me." For instance, fourteen-year-old Kelsey lies by telling her friends that she spent a lot of money on her designer coat when in reality her mom got it at a thrift store for a few dollars. She's afraid to be honest, believing that her friends might think less of her if they knew the truth. Roger is seven years old and feels bad that he takes regular medication. He tries to hide the fact and even tells his friends that he goes to the nurse's office because she is his friend and he is just saying hi.

Another reason children lie is to gain attention. They exaggerate stories or make things up to impress others. After all, the person who tells a good story is listened to and appreciated. If a child doesn't have a real story to tell, the temptation is to create one. Lying can be a way to gain attention by having a bigger story than someone else.

It is hurtful, confusing, and frustrating when a child lies. Instead of reacting in anger, take some time to recognize what's going on and then begin to develop a plan that focuses on honesty. Lying is wrong, but behavior change is not enough. We want more than truthful words. We want our children to develop integrity.

LANGUAGE WITHOUT LOGIC

Many young children confuse fantasy with truth. They have a hard time knowing the difference between their desires and the facts. For example, Tyler, age three, believes that his thoughts are reality. He may be angry at his sister, Kelly, and even wish she would get hurt. When Kelly does get injured, Tyler feels guilty. He believes he caused the injury by thinking unkind thoughts. For young children, reality and thoughts get confused, and logic has nothing to do with the equation.

In their creativity and immaturity, these kids sometimes tell stories that aren't true. Sometimes preschoolers, for instance, tell stories as truth because they *wish* the story were true. Or a child who tries to tell a story without having all the facts may make up the details she doesn't understand or remember. Her brain has a hard time recognizing the difference between what actually happened and what details she is filling in.

One day I (Joanne) was talking with a three-year-old girl. When she showed me her stuffed animal kitten, I asked her if she had a real cat.

"Yes, in the garage," she replied.

"How many cats do you have?" I pursued.

"One, two, three, four, five!" she pronounced proudly.

I smiled and continued the conversation. "Do you have any brothers or sisters?"

"Yes. I have a sister."

Knowing my new friend had two sisters, I asked, "How many sisters do you have?"

"One, two, three, four, five!" she pronounced just as confidently as before.

I was beginning to get the picture. I imagine any question with the words "How many?" would probably receive the same reply. As young children grow and develop, they think differently than adults. The facts may seem obvious to you, but they aren't so clear to your child.

In these instances, the child doesn't intend to deceive, but it is important to teach the child the difference between what is true and what is not. Four-year-old Jenny tells her cousin that she has a friendly lion living in her basement. As Mom hears Jenny telling the story, she can gently say, "Jenny, I think you need to start your story, 'I wish I had a friendly lion in my basement, and here's what it would be like.'" When Sammy, age five, starts telling the fictitious story about how he lived on a sailboat all summer, Dad might help his son start the story,

"Wouldn't it be interesting if I lived the whole summer on a sailboat?" These children don't necessarily need a rebuke for lying, but they do need guidance in their creativity to learn how to properly guard the truth as they speak creatively.

Young children need consistent and patient training. Listen carefully to what your kids say to distinguish lying from immaturity.

Too Much Truth Can Be Hurtful

Parents need to help their children know when and how to speak the truth. Keeping a secret without lying can be difficult. A mom may feel frustrated with her daughter, for example, who tells her brother what he's getting for Christmas. Mom didn't want her to tell the truth in that situation.

Another mom said, "I can hardly wait for my son to get out of this four-year-old stage where he says whatever he's thinking. It's so embarrassing. Just yesterday we were at the park and Ryan saw a man who was smoking and walking his dog. Ryan wanted to pet the dog, so we went over and began a conversation. Ryan looked up at the man and said, 'If you smoke you get cancer,' leaving me wanting to hide behind a tree. Last week he asked a girl at the grocery store why her hair looked funny."

Four-year-olds are notorious for telling the whole truth…and a little more. Tangents are the norm, and most four-year-olds have a story to go along with anything you have to say. One teacher of a four-year-old Sunday school class told the mom of an outspoken student, "I promise not to believe all the stories your daughter tells me about home if you promise not to believe all the stories she tells you about me."

Children must learn how and when to share the truth, and when to keep quiet. Just because children know something, that doesn't mean they should say it. Having the truth and presenting it are two different things. This isn't just a lesson for young children. Teens and adults also must learn this skill. Ephesians 4:15 tells us to speak the truth in love. Galatians 6:1 says, "If someone is caught in a sin, you who are spiritual should restore him gently." Sometimes having the truth isn't the only prerequisite for presenting it. Gentleness and discretion are also necessary. Teaching children to tell the truth is important, but it's not enough. They also need to understand acceptable ways to present it.

HONESTY IS MORE THAN TELLING THE TRUTH

Lying is a sign of a character weakness. It's a shortcut. Greed and impulsiveness set a person up for dishonesty. A child who lies sacrifices a clear conscience for some kind of immediate gain. He exchanges godly values for a quick-fix solution.

Ultimately, lying comes from our sin nature; it's a heart problem. Only through salvation in Christ can we fully live out a commitment to the truth. As parents, we must pray that the daily work we do with our kids will set the stage for a deeper work of God's grace in their lives. The work of parenting can only prepare a child for right thinking and acting. God is the one who changes the heart. The Holy Spirit uses parents to teach and train for godliness, so the effort you give to helping your child develop integrity will go a long way.

Character Foundations

The strategies for dealing with dishonesty in children start with more than just stressing telling the truth. Three foundational character qualities are usually weak in kids who struggle in this area. These qualities need reinforcement.

First, children who succumb to lying often lack *contentment.*

They seem to want more than they have, and they want it faster than is possible. Contentment is the ability to be happy with what you have instead of longing for what you don't have. Contentment believes that I'm okay and that people like me for who I am. I don't have to pretend things to make myself more acceptable or likeable. First Timothy 6:6 says, "Godliness with contentment is great gain." Contentment allows children to be happy with who they are, what they know, and what they can and cannot do. It teaches a child to live within limits so that she is able to accept a no answer and not lie to get what she is not allowed to have. Helping children understand and develop contentment can free them up to be more comfortable with the truth.

Contentment often comes through "in-life" discussions about what happiness is and the futility of seeking greener pastures. Contentment may come by parents being less permissive and saying no more often. When a child always has to have the latest thing or a bigger or better toy, something's wrong. Inadvertently, some parents, in an attempt to love their children, give them too much. Seeing that saying no provokes anger, they conclude that if they say yes more often a child will avoid an anger problem. Unfortunately, indulgence doesn't satisfy but often creates a desire for more and more. Contentment comes when a child learns to live within limits.

A second character quality that helps a child learn to be honest is *self-control.* Children often lie impulsively because it's easier. Children think if they lie, they can avoid negative consequences, so they say, "I didn't do it." Self-control helps a child learn to think before speaking, evaluate what's right, and respond with honesty rather than trying to take the easy way out. Controlling one's impulses is a sign of maturity and will prevent some of the "spur of the moment" temptation to use deception to get something or avoid consequences.

Self-control can be taught in a number of ways, some of which are suggested in chapter 7. Lying is a shortcut that children take because the long way looks too hard. Self-control helps children resist the urge to cut corners. Look for ways to help your kids develop the inner control necessary to be successful at handling temptation in life.

Responsibility is a third character quality that is necessary for developing honesty. It's the ability to abide by family values even when no one is watching. That means children tell the truth even when no one will know the difference. The essence of integrity is being the same person on the inside that people see on the outside. Responsibility chooses to act with integrity when no one is checking because you know in your heart that what you're doing in secret is what determines who you are. The person who is responsible can remember a task, complete it, and report back without being reminded. A responsible person can be honest under pressure. This internal commitment to honesty is a part of maturity that, unfortunately, many adults have grown up without.

Responsibility is taught with a short leash. Some parents give their children too many privileges too early. Use of a cell phone, access to the Internet, or freedom to stay home alone while Mom goes shopping can be deadly privileges for a child who isn't ready to handle them. Give small opportunities to be responsible and talk about them. Check up on children who are sent to do a task. Inspect their work to see if they have done it thoroughly and completely. Praise them for a job well done. Point out early indications of responsibility and use them to build a sense of trustworthiness in life.

When children demonstrate maturity and responsibility, they can enjoy more freedom. Age alone doesn't bring privileges; freedom needs to be earned. Just because some twelve-year-olds can stay home alone doesn't mean that your child can. Be careful about comparing your children to those in other families. The neighbors may allow their kids to watch movies that are not appropriate for your child. Teach your children that they can earn the privileges and freedoms they want by demonstrating character and maturity.

Getting to the Root of the Problem

One dad said, "Our son had a problem with lying when he was younger. We used to force him to restate his words to tell the truth. That wasn't enough. We began to realize that the issue was more than words and that we needed a bigger plan. We recognized that lying was behavior that indicated a deeper problem in his heart. We started working on related character qualities and began to see some real improvement. He's ten years old now and has a strong commitment to honesty. He even challenges his mom and me in this area sometimes." Simply focusing on telling the truth may not be enough for a child who lacks integrity. Discipline your child for the issue at hand but look for other ways to develop character qualities such as contentment, self-control, and responsibility.

Another dad told us, "I felt shocked, hurt, and disappointed when I discovered that my seven-year-old son, Chad, was lying to me. I was completely overwhelmed and didn't know what to do. I began working on character on a number of levels. When I disciplined him I talked about integrity and trust: 'When you don't tell me the truth I feel disappointed because I have always been able to depend on what you say and mean.' Over several months I began to see honesty more and more. It's been a few years now, but I'm feeling confident that I can trust Chad again."

Helping your child develop and rely on a personal relationship with God will encourage integrity. When children have a desire to please the Lord, not just people, their actions are different and their decisions reflect thoughtfulness. As you help your children develop a commitment to integrity, you are touching much more than behavior. You are addressing their private lives, a place where they often believe no one is watching. But what happens in secret is eventually revealed in behavior. Integrity helps children put their private lives in order and prepares them to live honest lives before others and with God.

HONESTY AS A LIFESTYLE

You can do many things to help your child develop honesty as a lifestyle. Here are nine suggestions for working with children who have a problem with lying.

1. Explore Honesty at Different Stages

Young children need to learn the difference between fantasy, pretend, wishes, teasing, filling in the gaps, misinformation, joking, exaggeration, and the real truth. Take your child's developmental stage into account when you hear statements that aren't true. Determine whether you're dealing with deliberate lying or immaturity. What is your child's intent? What's he trying to communicate? Help your children by prefacing your statements of make-believe or by debriefing after a time of joking or stories so that kids can clearly see the line between real and pretend. Tell and read stories that are true as well as those that are make-believe and ask your children the question, "Do you think this story is true or pretend?" Ask the same question after the stories that they tell you.

As children get older, dialogue about ethical dilemmas in life. Knowing when and how to tell the truth can be complicated, and even teens benefit from interacting with these ideas. Help your children understand what lying is and challenge them to develop a commitment to integrity.

2. Teach Children to Work Hard

Truth takes effort. It requires an inner commitment to take the long way instead of a shortcut. A child may sweep the dirt under a rug or report a job done that is incomplete in order to get out of work. Those are shortcuts. Why would anyone want to take the longer way? Because the long way facilitates a clear conscience. The child who stuffs his clothes under the bed when asked to clean up his room is taking a shortcut but has to live with guilt and fear. Working hard to do the job right isn't easy, but it has the lasting reward of a clear conscience.

The idea of working hard to address dishonest character comes from the Bible. Ephesians 4:28 gives excellent advice for dealing with someone who steals (another form of dishonesty). "He who has been stealing must steal no longer, but must work, doing something useful with his own hands, that he may have something to share with those in need." A child who learns to work hard gains a sense of accomplishment and sees he can be successful without taking a shortcut. He experiences the pride of earning something in an honest way instead of taking it dishonestly. Hard work helps build character. Children need to learn to work hard, and they should be given chores around the house. They may also benefit from music lessons and joining sports teams. Look for ways to encourage your children to give their best and press on to complete a job fully.

3. Monitor Closely

Children who have a problem with dishonesty need you to watch them more, check up on them often, and limit them when it comes to tempting opportunities. As a parent, you need to follow up on their stories. Take the long way home to drive by the school where your daughter is supposed to be. Drop by the friend's house to see if your son is really doing what he said. Make the extra phone call just to check. You don't have to be secret about it. Your child should know that you are checking. One dad said, "At first I felt like a spy, but now it's no secret. I'm just doing my job as a dad. My son knows that I could show up at any time, and I do. I take time to meet his friends and see how he's doing. Sometimes he acts like I'm an irritation, so I try to be sensitive and caring, not acting as a policeman. It's actually turned out to be a good thing because it's opened up conversations between the two of us about his friends and activities. Most importantly, it's developed a sense of accountability between us, and he knows that I want him to succeed. I'm not trying to catch him lying. I'm trying to confirm that he's telling the truth. He's actually earning the respect and integrity we both want for him."

Monitoring our children teaches them responsibility. Even children who are usually honest may try out lying to see what they can get away with. Be there to catch them. Let them know that lying doesn't pay. Some parents feel they should trust their children, believing the best. That may be true for adults we love, but children are immature and may not have the skills they need. We can't just assume they've got the honesty skill down. They may need some help and training. We don't simply imagine that our children know how to clean their bedrooms; we teach and then we check up. The same is true with honesty. We train and need to check up occasionally to make sure they're doing okay. Children may complain, "You don't trust me." Your reply is "I love you and want to help you be trustworthy." Trust is earned.

4. Treat Privacy as a Privilege

The child who lies needs greater accountability. She needs to be caught more often. Sometimes a child believes that her bedroom is off limits to parents or that the Web sites she visits are no one else's business. Parents might believe that privacy is a right and hesitate to check up on their kids. One mom said, "I went into my son's room to put away some clothes and couldn't believe what I saw. He had offensive magazines in his drawer. I didn't know what to do. I felt like I had violated his privacy and that I should have stayed out of his room. On the other hand, I knew that what he was doing was wrong. He was in great danger, and I needed to confront him."

Privacy is not a right. It's a privilege. One of the temptations for children struggling with lying is that they believe they can do things in secret. That child needs less privacy, not more. Privacy is earned when a child is trustworthy. It doesn't come with age. A child who is not honest may not have the privilege of a bedroom door, for instance. Children need to realize that they can never be completely alone anyway because God is always watching. Tell your children you'll be checking on them. Let them know that you'll be in and out of the room while they're on the phone and that you monitor their email. Don't allow privacy to be a stumbling block for a child who struggles with dishonesty. It can provide the opportunity for your child to fail.

5. Take Strong Action for Offenses

Teach children that lying isn't a shortcut; it's painful. When you discover that your daughter has lied, discipline her. Confrontation is an important part of the correction process, but don't stop there. Choose consequences that contribute to character or look for ways to have your child do restitution. When other people are involved, require an apology. One mom discovered that her son had lied to his coach about being too sick to practice soccer. "It was hard for me and for my son to go back to the coach, but we did. My son cried as he admitted what he had done. I felt like crying myself. The experience was a good deterrent for him. I don't think he'll try that again."

One dad and mom discovered that their fourteen-year-old daughter was lying. When her teacher gave her a detention after school, she told her parents that she was staying with a friend that day. When her parents found out, they not only disciplined their daughter at home, but they also spoke with her teacher and her guidance counselor about the incident. "We made a strong statement that day that we weren't going to tolerate the deception and that the consequences were bigger than she ever imagined. That incident had a dramatic effect, and we have seen a marked change in her over the past couple of years."

Dishonesty is a serious problem. Children need to see that lying just digs the hole deeper. You may not feel that your situation requires calling a guidance counselor or teacher, but maybe you should consider getting others involved in your child's life. Some parents try to keep family secrets to themselves and are afraid to get outside help for fear of damaging their reputation. A family that pretends to be good on the outside while hiding problems on the inside is living a lie. It's usually humbling to get outside help for your children, but don't let your pride prevent you from providing your kids with the training they need. School and church counselors, youth leaders, and coaches provide adult leadership that communicates the importance of integrity in relationships.

6. Teach About Honesty

Another way to help your kids be more honest is to teach honesty in daily life. Make observations in life from things you read in the newspaper or from stories you hear. Life is full of situations that require people to decide how they will deal with truth. Many people lie because they think it's the easy way out, only to find out later that the consequences are terrible.

With young children you might read stories like *The Emperor's New Clothes* or *The Boy Who Cried Wolf* and discuss the issues involved. Teach children how to know when to tell the truth and when to keep quiet, what a lie is and how to avoid lying even in the most difficult of situations.

When my (Scott) children were young, Carrie created an "Honest Under Pressure Award." A special sign was placed on a child's door when that child demonstrated integrity in a difficult situation. It might be admitting a mistake or taking responsibility for a job poorly done or just telling the truth when it wasn't easy. Carrie gave a visual reward for these acts of honesty, helping all of us see the importance of integrity.

Memorize Bible verses and discuss stories from the Scriptures about people who lied or told the truth in difficult situations. Develop a family prayer life to address some of the significant problems your family faces. Ask God to show you what it means to have integrity in the midst of challenging situations. Share with your kids the opportunities you have as an adult to make choices that reveal character.

7. Become a Human Lie Detector

Learn to detect when your kids are lying. This requires that you know your children. Pay attention to what they're saying and what they're doing. Are they open with you about their friends and their activities? Have regular conversations just to get to know them better as they grow and change. Build positive relationships that foster openness. Take an interest in their lives. Learn to listen to their words and their actions. This will help you know how and when to check out their stories.

Some children are very good at covering their tracks, and dishonesty can become quite an art for them, particularly as they get older. Preschool children can lie with words but often don't have the nonverbal cues to convince someone else that they're telling the truth, making it easier for parents to discern a dishonest statement. Little

Alex may say that he didn't eat the candy, but the way he shifts his body and avoids eye contact reveals his guilt.

By the time children reach older elementary age (ten to twelve years old), however, they develop more sophisticated communication skills and are often able to convince others with both words and non-verbal cues. At this age, Alex might leave you wondering whether or not he really ate the candy. He has become quite convincing until you notice that he left the wrapper in his wastebasket. If a habit of lying persists, an older child can turn lying into a lifestyle, making it very difficult to see through the dishonesty. As a teenager, Alex may be so convincing that you even feel guilty considering that he took the candy. He leads you to believe that he would never think of doing such a thing.

Take time to pray and ask God to reveal small indicators that something is wrong. You will be surprised at how many times you'll discover the truth in unexpected ways. One mom said, "I pray that God will show me right away when my kids are doing the wrong things, and he does. I want to take action quickly to prevent a problem from getting worse."

8. Teach About the Benefit of the Doubt

People are usually assumed to be honest and trustworthy until they prove themselves otherwise. Once trust is broken, however, it takes a person quite awhile to earn back that trust. Losing the benefit of the doubt is the natural consequence of lying. A person who lies one time develops a reputation of being a liar.

Help children understand that losing the benefit of the doubt is a sad and serious consequence. Build a vision for honesty by talking about the rewards. Show your kids ways to earn trust back and coach them in the process.

9. Be Trustworthy Yourself

Your children will learn about honesty from you in more ways than you might be willing to admit. Sometimes a child is told when a phone rings to "Tell them I'm not home." When you see parents passing their children off as a younger age to get cheaper theater tickets, you know that the parents are training those kids in the art of dishonesty. If you're invited to a social event and don't want to go, your child makes note of what you tell the person who calls.

Truth is the difference between integrity and hypocrisy. If you want your children to develop a commitment to integrity, you must model it. What do you do when the cashier makes a mistake and gives you extra change? How do you respond when given a difficult situation where a lie could relieve the pressure? If you have a commitment to integrity, your children will learn that a clear conscience is worth the extra effort. Remember that trust is necessary for strong relationships. Be trustworthy with your children.

Life provides many awkward and confusing predicaments. Use them to teach your children the value of a life of honesty. Your trustworthiness with your children will ease the relationship building process with them and help them develop lives of integrity.

WHAT ABOUT THE THINGS I CAN'T PROVE?

Living with a child who is dishonest is not easy. You're always second-guessing her, wondering if she's lying again. Sometimes you suspect that your son is doing the wrong thing, but you can't prove it. He may deny it, and there doesn't seem to be anything you can do.

In those moments, be careful not to push too hard. Don't try to force a confession or prove something you can't. After all, your child may be innocent this time, and you don't want to overemphasize a lack of trust. Remember that a child who lies will provide you with a number of opportunities to confront. That's an unfortunate reality, but it means that you don't have to press an unclear situation. You can wait for one that is clearer and determine to make an issue out of it at that time. Other times, you might simply make an observation about the importance of honesty and move on.

One mom told a story from her childhood. "I remember one time when Dad called all six of us kids into the room. He asked who broke the lamp. No one said a word. Dad became angry and pushed harder; still no one confessed. Finally Dad threatened to punish all of us if someone didn't admit to breaking the lamp. He was furious. I remember my little sister starting to cry. She said she did it. Looking back, I don't think she really broke the lamp. She just wanted to relieve the tension. She often tried to keep the peace in that way. I now realize that Dad was merely looking for someone to blame. Unfortunately, I don't think we learned anything about honesty or confession in those 'group sessions.'"

Children often lie to get out of trouble. They need to learn that lying is more painful than truth. When children struggle with dishonesty, we need to teach them that telling the truth is actually more rewarding. As children get older, we want them to readily confess their sins to God instead of trying to cover them up. Now is the time for them to learn. Openness and honesty with God start with our relationships at home. The goal is for our kids to develop a lifestyle of honesty, but when they fail, they need to be able to confess and feel forgiven.

Look for ways to correct on the spot, but also use lying as a cue that you have some greater work to do in the character department. As you teach, correct, and pray for your children who have lied, you will be working along with God to develop a heart of integrity in them. Your investment will be worth it in the end.

PUTTING IT ALL TOGETHER

When You See...

Lying, take action, but don't assume that correcting is enough. Children who resort to deception also need character training.

Move into a Routine...
1. Explore Honesty at Different Stages
2. Teach Children to Work Hard
3. Monitor Closely
4. Treat Privacy as a Privilege
5. Take Strong Action for Offenses
6. Teach About Honesty
7. Become a Human Lie Detector
8. Teach About the Benefit of the Doubt
9. Be Trustworthy Yourself

Because...

You are not just correcting a child for making a false statement. You are building character and teaching about the importance of integrity. God is more concerned with an honest heart than with behaviors that just look good on the outside.

QUESTIONS FOR FURTHER DISCUSSION

1. What is one thing you learned about lying from the Lie Detector Test at the beginning of this chapter?
2. Discuss the statement, "Honesty is foundational to relationships." What does this mean and why is honesty so important?
3. How can a child earn back trust?

DIGGING DEEPER

1. Read Genesis 20:1-12. Why did Abraham lie (verse 11)? How did he justify it in his own mind (verse 12)? What effect did it have on Abimelech when he found out (verses 4-5)?

2. Read Daniel 3:10-18. Why did the young men refuse to worship the image of gold? What lessons about integrity can be learned from their example?

3. Read Acts 5:1-10. Why do you think Ananias and Sapphira lied? Who did they lie to (verse 4)? What can children learn from this story?

4. Read Ephesians 4:15. What does it mean to speak the truth in love? Does it mean we compromise truth?

BRINGING IT HOME

Use the Lie Detector Test at the beginning of this chapter to engage your children in discussions about honesty and how to handle difficult situations. Don't try to cover all of them in one sitting. Remember that the tangents and conversations you have may be more important teaching opportunities than covering all the material. A commitment to integrity is learned over time.

9

*Be kind and compassionate to one another, forgiving
each other, just as in Christ God forgave you.*
Ephesians 4:32

"I'm Still Angry"

Forgiveness:
Living the Gift of Peace

Dear Scott and Joanne,

I knew my anger was damaging relationships with my kids, but
it seemed as if I had no other choice. Over the years I've tried
to control the outbursts, but when life got busy or I felt overwhelmed, I'd do it again. I heard myself yelling but couldn't seem
to stop. I felt like a volcano that, once erupting, just kept going.

I've tried some of the strategies you teach about helping children learn to accept no for an answer and teaching them to follow instructions. It's helped some, but I still get so angry. I don't
like it, and I know my kids are frightened sometimes. Frankly, I'm
frightened too.

When I heard you both teaching about forgiveness, something
struck me. I thought I had dealt with my past and grown beyond
the pain and disappointment. I see now how my frustrations and

unmet expectations with my kids just feed the bitterness I've accumulated. I know it's time to learn more about forgiveness so I can really move on.

Thank you for giving me hope. I believe that with God's strength and direction I will be able to change. I pray that as I grow I'll learn to deal with each day's frustrations in a healthy way and not carry the pain and anger around with me or vent it on my children.

—Kendra from Little Rock, Arkansas

We've spent most of this book looking for ways to change your family's relational routines in order to reduce your angry responses and help your children develop maturity. But you may still be feeling angry. What is it that causes you to react so quickly or move to anger so fast? If you know the answer, you can probably adapt one of the previous chapters to your situation and develop plans to make necessary changes.

If, however, you still see yourself with more anger than you expected, you'll most likely find this chapter helpful. It's here that we want to deal with stored-up anger. Living with accumulated anger can cause you to react more quickly and more intensely than the current problem warrants. If you find yourself angry much of the time, maybe you need to look at some of your own patterns for dealing with frustrating situations.

You can deal with your anger by practicing more patience and implementing the routines in this book. Most daily offenses are small enough that you can deal with them without harboring anger. Cleaning out your anger tank each night before you go to bed is always the healthiest thing to do.

Other offenses, however, have deeper roots and must be handled carefully. Sometimes people collect anger over time because of significant hurts that are too big to shrug off. These hurts accumulate on the bottom of your internal anger tank and make you more prone to anger on a daily basis.

God has provided solutions for doing deep cleaning in your life. So grab a cup of tea, make yourself comfortable, and fasten your seat belt. This chapter may stir up some old feelings and will hopefully give you a godly way of handling them. By going through the process we've outlined, you will understand more clearly how to deal with bigger offenses on a regular basis to prevent them from becoming lingering problems. You will also be able to help your children know how to respond to the hurts they experience so they can avoid carrying around unresolved pain as they get older.

THE BITTERNESS FORMULA

Anger is usually caused by pain of one sort or another. As we know, everyone experiences pain. People disappoint us. Expectations are dashed. Hopes are left unfulfilled. Life is unfair. Many people respond to this pain by blaming others and seeking revenge through anger. If they can't find someone to blame, they may turn their anger on God or just become angry at life itself. When you repeatedly respond to pain with anger, you become bitter. A formula might look like this:

Hurt + Anger = Bitterness

Anyone who has experienced hurt can develop bitterness. We see it regularly in couples going through a divorce, in families where teens have gone astray, and in relationships when adults and children have experienced some significant loss in their lives like the death of a loved one or the pain of living with a hurtful person. But bitterness can also accumulate through many small offenses. A wife may become bitter that her husband doesn't help around the house or that her children don't appreciate her. A father may become bitter because he doesn't like his job or because life has become harder than he expected. In chapter 2, we discussed the fact that anger is good. Bitterness, however, is anger misused.

You can tell when an adult or child is developing bitterness because their angry outbursts seem exaggerated. The person often vents accumulated anger on people in a way that's more frequent and intense than the problems seem to call for. Bitterness also causes a person to have a longer than normal recovery time after a hurtful experience. If you see these symptoms in yourself, it's time to take a deeper look to see if you are storing bitterness in your heart.

One dad said, "While I don't rant and rave, I did notice that I was becoming less tolerant of little annoyances and snapping at my kids. When I saw my children wilt right in front of my eyes and say things like 'I was just trying to…,' I realized I was overreacting to them. I saw that I was developing some bitterness toward my children, and I determined to deal with it."

Bitterness is not inevitable. We all know people who have experienced tremendous suffering yet haven't become resentful. In order to deal with bitterness you must separate the two ingredients, hurt and anger. So, first, we're going to look at God's plan for dealing with hurt and pain, and then we're going to look at his plan for dealing with anger.

FINDING HEALING FROM PAIN THROUGH COMFORT

When we are in pain we long to be comforted. Some people find comfort in alcohol or food or by drowning themselves in entertainment. Others go to friends or a quiet retreat setting to find peace and restoration. Anger can be deceptively comforting when we need a way to react to a painful situation.

Some habits of receiving comfort are more effective than others. Take, for example, two four-year-old boys who respond to their pain differently. Whenever Jason hurts his ankle, scrapes his knee, or bumps his head, he gets angry. He starts throwing things, yelling, and even hitting his parents.

Nine Ways to Exasperate Your Children

Exasperate is the opposite of comfort. Exasperated children get so frustrated that they become overly discouraged and want to give up hope. Watch out for these nine things that can exasperate your children and lead to bitterness.

1. Overprotecting them and not allowing them to learn from experience
2. Comparing children or showing favoritism
3. Treating them as if they are younger than they are
4. Neglecting or physically abusing them
5. Using bitter words and being demanding or impatient with them
6. Failing to listen to their feelings or desires
7. Wanting your children to succeed where you failed and imposing your goals on them
8. Being critical
9. Basing acceptance on what they do instead of who they are

When Zachary hurts his ankle, scrapes his knee, or bumps his head, he runs to his mom for comfort. He cries and crawls up on her lap. She holds him and comforts him. The comfort that Zachary receives helps him deal with the pain that he's experienced until it subsides. Zachary is then able to go back and live life without the lingering effects of anger.

God wants us to turn to him for comfort the way Zachary turns to his mother. That means that we learn to bring our pain to the Lord, trust him with our hurts, and accept his care on a daily basis. Through prayer and Scripture reading we learn more of his character and the ways in which he loves us. Knowing how to experience God's comfort is the first step in any plan for dealing with bitterness.

Receiving comfort is risky because it requires vulnerability. Zachary, who comes running to his mom for comfort, may get a lecture or criticism. You may have had a similar experience as a child and decided that it was too dangerous to ask for comfort from God or anyone else.

Sometimes earthly forms of comfort disappoint us. The best care comes from God himself. Look at the following passage from 2 Corinthians 1:3-7 (emphasis added):

> Praise be to the God and Father of our Lord Jesus Christ, the Father of compassion and the God of all *comfort,* who *comforts* us in all our troubles, so that we can *comfort* those in any trouble with the *comfort* we ourselves have received from God. For just as the sufferings of Christ flow over into our lives, so also through Christ our *comfort* overflows. If we are distressed, it is for your *comfort* and salvation; if we are *comforted,* it is for your *comfort,* which produces in you patient endurance of the same sufferings we suffer. And our hope for you is firm, because we know that just as you share in our sufferings, so also you share in our *comfort.*

If you don't have much experience allowing God or others to comfort you, maybe it's time to learn. God helps us receive and give comfort in our earthly relationships as we learn to receive comfort from him. One of the benefits of being a child of God is free access to his comfort. It's like finding out that because you married a doctor you now have free medical care. You may need to explore a new, healthy understanding of who God is and how to receive the comfort that comes from a relationship with him.

FINDING HEALING FROM ANGER THROUGH FORGIVENESS

Now let's talk about stored-up anger, especially the kind that's a response to pain in your life. Anger is often used as a coping mechanism for dealing with hurt because it has a way of covering up hurt so that you don't feel it. But anger is not a godly solution for dealing with pain and has some unwanted side effects.

There is a tool that removes bitterness by surgically separating the anger that has fused to your pain. That tool is forgiveness. Forgiveness detaches the anger from the hurt and prevents bitterness from accumulating. Removing the anger is scary, though, because it leaves the pain open and vulnerable. Many find that pain unbearable. That's why it is so important to learn how to receive the comfort of God. Understanding and trusting in God's comfort makes forgiveness an easier process.

Even when we learn how to embrace the comfort of God, however, we need to know what forgiveness is before we can implement it. Many people have a hard time with the concept of forgiveness because they don't understand what it really means. It's important to identify some common misconceptions about forgiveness and why they are not true.

Misconception 1: Forgiveness Requires Forgetting

We've heard a single mom say, "I can't forgive my ex-husband for all the hurt he's caused our family. I know I'm supposed to forgive and forget, but I also know that's impossible. The pain has scarred my life, and I will never forget it, so forgiveness is not an option for me."

This woman was making a big mistake because she had the misconception that forgiveness requires forgetting. There is no doubt that a difficult marriage or a divorce brings a tremendous amount of pain into a person's life. It's in these kinds of situations where forgiveness and healing are needed the most.

In Jeremiah 31:34 God tells Jeremiah, "I will forgive their wickedness and will remember their sins no more." Forgetting in the context of forgiveness doesn't mean "removing from memory." Rather, it means "not holding it against the offender." It isn't consistent with God's character to forget anything. God doesn't remember our sins in the sense that he doesn't hold them against us.

With God as our model we are free from the obligation to forget wrongs done to us. In fact, God uses our memory of past pain in our lives to increase our ability to minister to others. Second Corinthians 1:3-4 says that our God is the "God of all comfort, who comforts us in all our troubles, so that we can comfort those in any trouble with the comfort we ourselves have received from God." By experiencing the healing of God's comfort and remembering what he healed us from, we have more resources to help others.

Misconception 2: Forgiveness Means That We Ignore the Sins of Others

This idea is often phrased like this: "Since I am a Christian, and God wants me to overlook offenses, I should act as if this person has not sinned against me." Ignoring is actually the opposite of forgiving. Ignoring is pretending that the offense is not there; forgiveness acknowledges the offense. Ignoring leaves no room for confrontation; forgiveness opens the door for a wise confrontation.

God doesn't expect us to be passive Christians, doormats for others to abuse. Rather, God expects us to wisely take a stand for righteousness, helping others grow in their maturity as well. Anger blurs our ability to confront. In fact, it's best to confront the offender only after we have forgiven and removed the anger from our hearts.

One dad told us, "I thought forgiving meant I would have to ignore my son's offenses and not deal with them. That didn't seem right, so I never applied this idea of forgiveness in our relationship. I used to be angry all the time when he made wrong decisions and acted selfishly. Now that I've learned to forgive, I can come to the problems with a clear head. I don't get so blown away by anger, and I'm able to confront him in a way that's helpful."

Misconception 3: Forgiveness Is Pretending It Doesn't Hurt

Some people believe they can't forgive because they're still in pain. They think they need to somehow move beyond the pain or pretend it's not there before they can release the offense. Some even think that Christians should be strong enough to not feel hurt. God invites us, though, to recognize our hurt and go to him for comfort. When we admit the pain and allow God to comfort us, we are freed up to forgive others. Forgiveness doesn't mean we pretend it doesn't hurt. In reality, the offenses of others often hurt us a great deal. Recognizing and admitting our pain is the first step to forgiving. Minimizing our pain, in fact, can hinder the process of forgiveness.

We know God forgives us, but we also know he grieves when we sin against him (Ephesians 4:30). Now, God is God, and his grief is different from ours, but the principle is the same. God forgives even though sin grieves him. We forgive even though others hurt us. Looking to God's model we see that true forgiveness requires that we are honest about the offense. One mom told us, "I used to be afraid of pain. I now realize that I was using anger as a way to cope with all the hurt I experienced from my kids, my parents, and my boss. I'm learning to view pain in a different way. Recognizing that God wants to comfort me has been helpful. When people do selfish things that hurt me, forgiveness means something different for me now. I realize that it's okay to admit I was hurt. I can deal with the problem on two fronts. I receive God's comfort to deal with my pain, and I can address the offense with the hurtful person. By separating the two, I feel much more at peace than I ever did before."

Misconception 4: Forgiveness Is a Once-for-All Experience

Some people feel guilty because they are still angry even after they have decided to forgive. When anger has accumulated over time, forgiveness isn't a one-time event. The smallest infraction by the offender might send your mind back to the anger department and cause your feelings to return. Then guilt sets in, you feel discouraged, and you are in the middle of another negative cycle.

In Luke 17, Jesus taught his disciples how to have a *lifestyle* of forgiveness. "If he sins against you seven times in a day, and seven times comes back to you and says, 'I repent,' forgive him" (verse 4). The disciples had a hard time with that statement and replied to the Lord, "Increase our faith!" (verse 5). Each time you forgive, you are taking a step of surrender to the Lord. Forgiveness goes against our natural human tendency to protect ourselves with anger. It's difficult to release the offense when you know that the offender may hurt you again, but when you trust God for comfort, you forgive out of obedience. The next moment or the next day may bring another similar opportunity. Forgiveness is not once for all. It is a way of life requiring faith.

It's not hard for most of us to relate to the idea of continual forgiveness. Just stop for a moment and ask yourself the question, "Who is one person who has hurt me deeply?" It's amazing how fast someone comes to your mind, isn't it? Or you may be driving along and hear a story on the radio that reminds you of the time you were treated unfairly by someone. You experience the emotions all over again, ready to give that person a piece of your mind. Forgiveness is a life-long project. You have to keep at it. One of the beautiful things about living a lifestyle of forgiveness is that when we surrender to God by forgiving someone else, his Spirit works in us to help us forgive more quickly and harbor anger less. Over time we are less burdened by the pain others cause us.

Misconception 5: Forgiveness Is Optional

As Christians, we have a calling. We are called to completely surrender to our Lord Jesus Christ. Suffering, persecution, and sacrifice are sometimes parts of the commitment we make. Forgiveness requires sacrificing our desire to seek revenge, allowing the Lord to judge others instead. He wants to direct our paths. In place of revenge and anger, we receive love, joy, and peace. Ephesians 4:32 tells us to be compassionate and to forgive. It's not an option. It's part of who we are in Christ. It's work. It's hard. It's a sacrifice, but what's new? That's what it means to be a child of God. The cost is great, but so are the rewards.

One mom said, "When I decided to give my life to the Lord, it was an amazing experience. I used to think I was a pretty good person and didn't need religion, but then I heard the information about Christianity a little differently than before. A friend told me that it isn't a list of dos and don'ts, but it's a relationship with Jesus, and that he would not only forgive me but also help me to forgive others. I knew my anger was turning me into an ugly person. My friend who was telling me all this seemed to be at peace. I wanted what she had, so I decided to give my life to Christ. I realize now that forgiveness is not an option. Not only is it something God has called me to do, but it even helps me to enjoy life to the fullest. I can't believe it took me so long to learn this. I just wasn't cut out to carry around all that anger. I have an amazing peace now."

So Then What Is Forgiveness?

Forgiveness is releasing the offense from your heart. It means letting go of the need to get justice in the situation and, when possible, looking for healthy solutions instead.

Holding on to anger makes you miserable. It clouds your vision and makes you critical and explosive with even the small frustrations of life. You end up seeing all of life in terms of your pain, causing you to become self-focused. You grow to be an unhappy and unpleasant person.

If, on the other hand, you forgive, you are able to release the anger and receive freedom inside. You no longer go around with something to prove or with the need to protect yourself or obtain justice. In short, you are free. Forgiveness is not just a good idea; it's necessary if you want to be healthy and, certainly, if you want to have healthy kids.

So how do you forgive? Sometimes you may feel like your pain has tied you into so many emotional knots that you don't even know where to start. God is gracious and gives quite a bit of instruction in his Word about how to forgive. In fact, we identify four general routes to forgiveness that the Bible offers us. You may discover that one of the routes suits your situation better than the others. You may also find that in certain cases, you need all four. Look at these four routes to forgiveness and pray that God will transform how you process hurt from your past and how you handle pain in your life now.

Route 1: Understand the Offender

In Luke 23:34, Jesus says, "Father, forgive them, for they do not know what they are doing." Jesus understood his attackers. He knew that they didn't realize they were pawns in Satan's hand. Because Jesus understood more about them and more about God than they did, he was able to forgive them. Deeper understanding is one of the routes that allows us to trust God and forgive someone who has hurt us.

One thirteen-year-old boy growing up in a single parent family was deeply hurt and needed very much to understand this concept of forgiveness. Our hearts went out to him because we could see what his anger was doing to him, even at his young age. We worked together in counseling for several weeks trying to communicate what forgiveness is and how to apply it to his life. We explained this route to forgiveness, and after a couple of weeks he told us, "I'm not as angry anymore. Whenever I start getting really mad, I try to think about why the person is doing what he's doing. I know he's not trying to hurt me intentionally but is just focusing on other things like greed or his own hurt or wanting attention, so he does things that are hurtful. I still don't like it, but it helps me to not take things so personally."

Route 2: Recognize Your Own Offenses

In Matthew 18:23-35, Jesus responds to Peter's question about forgiveness by telling a story about a servant who, forgiven a debt by his master, turned around and refused to forgive someone who owed him money.

> The kingdom of heaven is like a king who wanted to settle accounts with his servants. As he began the settlement, a man who owed him ten thousand talents was brought to him. Since he was not able to pay, the master ordered that he and

his wife and his children and all that he had be sold to repay the debt.

The servant fell on his knees before him. "Be patient with me," he begged, "and I will pay back everything." The servant's master took pity on him, canceled the debt and let him go.

But when that servant went out, he found one of his fellow servants who owed him a hundred denarii. He grabbed him and began to choke him. "Pay back what you owe me!" he demanded.

His fellow servant fell to his knees and begged him, "Be patient with me, and I will pay you back."

But he refused. Instead, he went off and had the man thrown into prison until he could pay the debt. When the other servants saw what had happened, they were greatly distressed and went and told their master everything that had happened.

Then the master called the servant in. "You wicked servant," he said, "I canceled all that debt of yours because you begged me to. Shouldn't you have had mercy on your fellow servant just as I had on you?" In anger his master turned him over to the jailers to be tortured, until he should pay back all he owed.

This is how my heavenly Father will treat each of you unless you forgive your brother from your heart.

The point of Jesus' story is that when we see how God has forgiven our great debt, we can more easily forgive someone else. Recognizing your own offenses becomes another route down the forgiveness path.

None of us is perfect. We probably all have people that are just as angry with us as we are with our offenders. We wish people would forgive us, give us a second chance, and believe the best in us, but we find it hard to do the same thing. Sometimes when we get angry with others it's helpful to humbly look at the people we have offended.

Route 3: Let God Be the Judge

Anger is a form of revenge. When you hold on to anger it hurts you and may even hinder God's work in the other person's life. Romans 12:17-21 is an excellent passage to memorize when struggling with anger and bitterness.

> Do not repay anyone evil for evil. Be careful to do what is right in the eyes of everybody. If it is possible, as far as it depends on you, live at peace with everyone. Do not take revenge, my friends, but leave room for God's wrath, for it is written: "It is mine to avenge; I will repay," says the Lord. On the contrary:
> "If your enemy is hungry, feed him;
>   if he is thirsty, give him something to drink.
> In doing this, you will heap burning coals on his head."
> Do not be overcome by evil, but overcome evil with good.

When you become bitter, in essence, you have taken the justice system into your own hands. You become the judge and jury, and your anger is the sentence against that person. God never intended for you to carry the burden of justice for the whole world or even the personal justice of your own life. Trusting God means that we leave justice in his hands.

Route 4: See the Benefits for You

When we fail to forgive, we are the ones who may suffer the most. In Matthew 5:23-24, Jesus warns that strained relationships hinder our worship.

Therefore, if you are offering your gift at the altar and there remember that your brother has something against you, leave your gift there in front of the altar. First go and be reconciled to your brother; then come and offer your gift.

In Matthew 6:14-15, Jesus connects our own forgiveness from God with our forgiveness of others.

For if you forgive men when they sin against you, your heavenly Father will also forgive you. But if you do not forgive men their sins, your Father will not forgive your sins.

Bitterness damages its owner more than it hurts the offender. It has a way of warping your personality and turning you into an unhappy person. When you're tempted to be a revenge-seeker or to harbor bitterness in your heart, stop and say to yourself, "This is just going to make me an ugly person." Look around in life at people you've grown up with or people you meet who have turned ugly inside because of their bitterness. Determine to address your anger now so you do not become like them.

God offers us many ways and reasons to forgive because bitterness is such a hard problem to overcome. Some people respond to one route to forgiveness better than another, while others need a crash course in all four at the same time. Spend time reading and thinking about the verses above. The Scriptures have a cleansing effect as we meditate on them; ask God to *wash* you with his Word.

You might want to create a forgiveness journal and go back to these truths and apply them daily to your experiences. Write down your prayers to God and reread the ones from the past. Be sure to note ways that God answered your prayers and helped you deal with the bitterness and resentment that you have felt.

The time and work you spend in this area will pay off. Remember that God is the one who changes hearts. We take steps of submission, but ultimately it is the supernatural touch of our loving heavenly Father that can change us for good. Anger can feel overwhelming at times, but we serve a God who heals, a God who cares, a God who loves. Take time to give this area of your life to the Lord. You won't be sorry.

HELPING CHILDREN WITH THEIR HURT AND PAIN

No matter how easy children's lives are, kids still experience pain. They may not realize how good they have it or how insignificant their pain is compared to other people's, but it's still real pain to them.

We've discovered a number of things you can do to help your children work through their hurt in godly ways and prepare them to prevent bitterness as they grow older. Bitterness is like a dirty house. You don't consciously choose it, but it happens over time if you don't have a plan to prevent it. A child's seemingly small hurt is the practice ground to learn how to deal effectively with hurt in life. As you tune in to your children's pain, you will have the opportunity to help them learn to process that pain in healthy ways.

Give Comfort

Some parents tell their kids to "Stop crying," "Grow up," or "Get over it" when their kids are sad or physically or emotionally hurt. Sometimes this encourages an angry response, which unfortunately is more socially acceptable than pain or tears. If children are going to learn to receive comfort from God, they must first learn how to receive comfort from Mom or Dad. Empathize with your children when they're hurt. After all, you're modeling the way that God comforts them. In Romans 12:15 Paul tells us to "mourn with those who mourn." You might say things like, "Ouch, I'll bet that hurts." Or, "I'd be sad if my friend did that to me too."

Sometimes parents move too quickly into a problem-solving mode before their child is ready. Children need to know that it's okay to feel sad and hurt and that getting alone, praying, crying on someone's shoulder, thinking about God's love, talking about the problem with you, or just allowing you to hold them quietly are all ways to receive comfort to deal with their pain. You may need to try all these ideas and more before you find the ones that minister to your child. That's okay. Take the time to experiment. In the process you may even learn more about comfort yourself.

Model Forgiveness

Sometimes parents see their own anger mirrored in their children. One dad said, "I was watching my daughter play with her friend. They got into an argument, and as Lauren got mad, I started feeling convicted. The way she yelled at her friend sounded all too familiar. I realized that I need to do some changing myself just to help her deal with her anger."

We can all learn more about giving and receiving forgiveness. Children should be able to look at their parents and see that they are working on it too. For instance, one son was surprised when his dad didn't retaliate when a teenager made an insulting remark in the bank parking lot. "Dad, why don't you get him back? That guy deserves to get yelled at."

"Son, I don't yell at people."

"Why not? He'll just keep getting away with it if you don't do something."

"I don't even know the guy. If I had an opportunity to correct him, I might, but I wouldn't do it by yelling at him. Most importantly, I don't want to let someone I don't even know make me angry inside. I have to let it go; otherwise, it will affect the rest of my day. Sometimes it's just not worth getting all upset about."

One mom rented a video for her kids to watch. Her daughter, who had not heard of the movie, went on and on about how boring the movie must be because of the title. Although Mom was feeling angry and unappreciated at the time, she didn't say anything. Later, she approached her daughter and said, "I felt hurt by the way you treated me about the video. I went out of my way to do something kind for you, and you don't even know what the video is about. You said several unkind things about it." Her daughter responded well and said, "Okay, I'm sorry, Mom." By responding with sorrow instead of anger, Mom modeled grief instead of revenge to her daughter.

Life provides many opportunities for us, as parents, to offer forgiveness. Children watch us live life and see that we face struggles similar to their own. Be transparent and model your own challenges as you forgive those who have offended you.

Look for Teachable Moments

Look at every anger situation as an opportunity to teach. First, empathize with your kids about the offense. "I can see why you're upset. That makes sense." Secondly, if the offender was wrong, validate that fact. This is helpful because children often feel that their anger is justified when the other person is wrong. By agreeing that the other person is wrong but still correcting for anger, the parent shows that a wrong action doesn't justify an angry outburst. Children need to understand that even if the other person is wrong, their own response is very important. "Your brother is wrong to have continued to tease you after you asked him to stop, but that doesn't justify your harsh words to him."

Third, talk about alternative responses. Children need to learn that sometimes they should confront and other times they should let the offense go. Verses like Galatians 6:1 help children see that confrontation isn't always the best choice: "Brothers, if someone is caught in a sin, you who are spiritual should restore him gently." Sometimes a child should not confront because she is not qualified to do so. It may be better to wait and watch for a better opportunity or even let someone else confront in a more effective way.

Some ways of confronting are more helpful than others. Children can talk about a problem, listen to another person, offer suggestions, get the help of a third party, or approach the problem indirectly by first appreciating the offender. These choices require skills, and your child may or may not be ready to tackle these kinds of relational issues. Regardless, harboring anger is not an option at any age. Kids need to learn to let offenses go so bitterness doesn't take root.

One mom heard some children in the neighborhood mistreating her son with verbal accusations and lies. She told her husband, who decided that he would go out and give those kids a piece of his mind. He was mad that they would treat his son that way. Dad went out and yelled at them and set the record straight. He won in the argument department but unfortunately lost in the relationship with his son. He got revenge at the expense of losing a good teaching opportunity about forgiveness and handling injustice in life. Confronting the children was a good idea, but it might have been handled better had he and his son discussed it first and then proceeded calmly with a plan.

Romans 12:18 is a great verse for children caught in relational problems: "If it is possible, as far as it depends on you, live at peace with everyone." You can't always change the other person, but you can control your response.

Kathy, a mother of two boys, ages eight and eleven, told us this story: "I remember the turning point for me last year. I was going off again, ranting and raving about one of my pet peeves—the boys' leaving things lying around the house instead of putting them away. I was mad and determined to let them know it. At some point in the process I looked at my older son and saw something in his eyes that made me stop. He was fearful and sad at the same time. I realized that I was modeling resentment. I wasn't just mad about today's problem. I was mad about all the days that I have to pick up after them. I had developed bitterness toward my kids. I know they're wrong. They should pick up and help out around the house, but that didn't justify my angry response.

"I determined to change. In fact, I explained to my kids the things I had learned about anger, forgiveness, and dealing with offenses. I told them they could help me with this by graciously pointing out when they feel I'm overreacting with anger. I agreed that I would try to respond in different ways. It's amazing what that has done to our relationship. I'm becoming less explosive, and my children are learning how to deal with offenses of others. This has been the greatest challenge of my life, but I am so grateful that I have a family where I can work out these things. God is teaching me more and more each day, and I just pray that I can help my children prevent some of what my poor anger management has put me through."

God gave us anger and other emotions to help us sense things about life. Those who save up anger out of self-protection, however, are making a mistake. By teaching your children how to receive comfort and how to give and receive forgiveness, you will equip them with tremendous skills that they will use for the rest of their lives.

But You Don't Know
What I've Been Through

Each person's pain is unique. What you've experienced may have pushed you to the limits of your ability to handle life. In painful times we all turn to coping strategies, but anger is only one way to deal with life's pain. You can't rely on excuses to remain angry. "I've had a hard life." "My parents were mean, divorced, absent, addicted…" "I was made this way." Life is hard and may have been harder for you than most. But many people have testimonies of how God turned their difficult past into something good. You can too. If you find yourself continually blaming your past, your heredity, or your painful experiences, you'll never get well. Now is the time to move on and learn to respond differently.

Forgiveness is one of those areas that's easier to talk about than to put into practice. Before you give up, though, take time to read and study God's Word. You may need the benefit of a good counselor to help you work through the application of forgiveness in your life, but don't forget that Jesus sent us the Holy Spirit to be our Counselor. John 14:26 says, "But the Counselor, the Holy Spirit, whom the Father will send in my name, will teach you all things and will remind you of everything I have said to you." Jesus told his disciples this knowing that he was going away and wouldn't be able to help them understand everything they would need to know. No better counselor can help you deal with anger and resentment than the Holy Spirit.

One mom, Gloria, said it this way: "Bitterness is like putting a cement block in front of your car before you drive away. You just can't get anywhere until you get rid of it. Prayer and a close relationship with God are the only ways to remove it." Sometimes God takes bitterness and resentment away miraculously, but many times God uses the daily work of sanctification to do the deep healing in our hearts. Overcoming bitterness and resentment takes time. Be patient with yourself and hang in there. God is at work. View your accumulated anger as an opportunity to give God another area of your life each day. The constant opportunities you have can be reminders that you are making Jesus Christ the Lord of your life again today.

PUTTING IT ALL TOGETHER

When You See...
Bitterness accumulating in your heart or in the lives of your children, look for ways to release it. Some of the signs of bitterness include over-reaction, exaggerated intensity, and an unhappy lifestyle.

Move into a Routine...
Separate the anger from the hurt and learn to deal with them God's way. Hurt is best addressed by receiving the comfort of God. Anger is released through forgiveness. Don't let misconceptions of forgiveness hinder you. Use suggestions from the Bible, such as understanding the offender, recognizing your own offenses, letting God be the judge, and seeing the benefit for you, as routes to forgiveness.

Because...
The alternative to forgiveness is an angry lifestyle. Angry responses are a form of revenge, and those who harbor bitterness are unhappy. Your

children need to understand how to deal with offenses in a healthy way. When parents model forgiveness, they also teach it.

QUESTIONS FOR FURTHER DISCUSSION

1. Review the five misconceptions about forgiveness. Which explanation do you find most helpful? Why?
2. Which of the four routes to forgiveness do you tend to rely on most? Why is it helpful?
3. Some children seem to be born with the temptation to accumulate anger. How can you tell a child is at risk for becoming bitter? What early steps can you take to prevent bitterness from growing?

DIGGING DEEPER

1. Look at Hebrews 12:14-15. How are the two commands in verse 14 related to the two commands in verse 15?
2. The book of Ruth tells a dramatic story of tragedy followed by amazing triumph. In the midst of the pain, Naomi returns home. Read what she said in Ruth 1:18-21. Who was she angry with and why? How is her situation like many today?
3. David is an excellent example of a man committed to avoiding bitterness. Read 1 Samuel 30:1-6 and answer the following questions. What pain did David's men experience? What pain did David experience from the enemy and also from his men? Contrast the response of the men with the response of David. Why do you think David was able to respond the way he did?

4. Read Acts 8:18-23. In Peter's rebuke he mentions that Simon was bitter. From the story in these verses, why do you think Simon might have been bitter? How might his actions have been connected to his bitterness?

BRINGING IT HOME

Inflate two balloons, one halfway and the other completely. Read the following: "Each person has an anger tank inside of them. The person whose tank is full of bitterness is always just about to pop."

Let your children squeeze the balloons and see the full one pop more easily. Read Ephesians 4:26,31-32. Together, answer the following question: What are some ways that you can clean bitterness out of your anger tank so that you don't explode so easily?

10

No discipline seems pleasant at the time, but painful.
Later on, however, it produces a harvest of righteousness
and peace for those who have been trained by it.
HEBREWS 12:11

The Gift No One Asks for but Everyone Needs

Dear Scott and Joanne,

I was talking with my mom the other day about the fact that I yell at my kids the same way she used to yell at my brother and me. She told me that my grandmother yelled at her and her siblings too. It's amazing what parents pass on without even realizing it.

I have one boy who is aggressively strong-willed, one who is passively strong-willed, and one who was more compliant—until he turned thirteen. When my boys were young I would yell. Maybe scream is more accurate. I didn't know how else I could get them to cooperate.

I always prayed for godly children, but then I started asking myself, "How can I expect my kids to be godly if they see their mom blowing up in anger all the time?" The Lord is teaching me to use consequences rather than arguments or yelling. By God's grace I don't react to my kids out of anger as much as I used to. One of my sons even remarked to me the other day that we aren't as angry as we used to be. I now have several constructive plans for helping them mature.

I still feel angry sometimes, but I'm not taking it out on my kids as much. They need a mom who can help them grow, not a volcano that's going to explode at any second. I'm learning to set firm limits and help the boys deal with conflict in a constructive way. We're all in this together, and I'm grateful to see how God is teaching my boys to follow him.

—Barb from Decatur, Florida

Many adults are committed to being good parents, and their devotion to loving relationships and family unity is admirable—but then comes the first baby. Often godly parents are surprised to discover that their child has a predisposition to meanness, selfishness, or defiance. One dad said, "How could this be? My wife and I love each other and want our home to be a pleasant, safe place—but our kids don't want to cooperate. It's no wonder I get angry—my children keep doing the wrong things!"

Parents want the best for their children. They want their home to be a place where peace reigns, love flourishes, and closeness grows and develops. Too often children don't cooperate. Parents work hard and make sacrifices for their kids but often see few, if any, signs of gratefulness. Patience is often answered by procrastination, and the parent's request for help is met with a bad attitude. Any hopeful expectations parents once had are shattered by the realities of actually living with children.

One mom said it this way: "Before I had children I used to imagine what it would be like to tuck my kids in at night. I'd go in and pat them on the head, kiss their forehead, turn off the light, and watch them blissfully drift off to sleep. WELL FORGET THAT! Bedtimes are a battle every night. Being nice doesn't work. I have to be mean or angry before they'll finally stay in their bedrooms."

Many parents are frustrated. They want more for their families and are eager to give the effort needed to make things work with less friction and more joy. Why, then, do they resort to yelling much of the time? Because yelling works. It gets things done. If your goal is to have your children come to the table, get in the car, or stop wrestling around, then overpowering them with harshness seems to do the job. But does it really? Yelling and harshness may get their attention, and may even get compliance, but it doesn't build the character or relational skills that children need.

Yelling is usually a sign that a parent doesn't have a plan. Imagine going to the car repair shop because of a problem with your brakes. After hours of work, the mechanic comes out and says, "We couldn't fix the brakes, so we just made your horn louder." Some parents are that way. They don't know how to fix the problems they have with their children, so they become louder, thinking that the intensity created through yelling will have some kind of positive effect. It doesn't work.

You might be saying, "Wait a minute! My kids won't obey unless I get angry." If that's true, maybe you've trained your children to respond to your anger as a signal that it's time to obey. How do your kids know when you're ready to stop talking, reminding, and nagging and that you're about to take some kind of action? Kids are smart. They know they can wait until the last minute before responding. They've figured out how many warnings you'll give, and they recognize the tone of voice that says you're ready to deliver a consequence.

The solution, in part, is to teach children to respond to a different cue. If yelling is the sign that you mean business, change the cue to a more constructive signal. If you teach your kids that you'll back up your words sooner, without anger, your dependency on anger to get things done will decrease.

Anger may produce results in the short-term, but over time, children learn to tune it out. One dad told us, "Initially, yelling got the attention of my kids. They did what I told them to do because they were afraid. Eventually the shouting resulted in their yelling back at me, and ultimately, yelling evoked no response—my children just ignored me."

Angry words might sometimes motivate children to do what you say, but a closer look reveals damaged family relationships. Short-term compliance comes at the cost of long-term closeness. Motivating with harshness can keep children in line or get them to accomplish a task but that method robs the family of joy. In the end, it is closeness that provides parents with teachable moments and the relaxed enjoyment of family life. Yelling and harshness discourage trust, essential to help young people learn valuable principles about life.

Good correction routines are helpful for both children and parents. Kids learn godly ways of handling mistakes when parents have a plan. If you know the routine, you're less likely to become emotionally upset and more likely to recognize that your persistence will produce character in the end. How you view your children and what you think about discipline can help you stay calm and use healthy routines when things get tough. Here are four tips.

1. CHILDREN ARE ON THE PRODUCTION LINE

Imagine a car dealership where a man named Martin works in the showroom. Martin sells cars to prospective customers. When he sees a car without a door, he's surprised and upset. He doesn't expect to see defects. Cars in the showroom are supposed to be finished.

Bill, on the other hand, works in the factory and inspects cars for flaws and missing parts. It's his job to find problems and fix them. In fact, Bill is prepared with a number of routines depending on the nature of the problem. If a door is missing, Bill doesn't get upset; he just goes through his routine of obtaining a door and putting it on. Bill knows that when a car is on the production line, it requires continual work. Doors are added, pieces are put together, and workers are continually looking for ways to improve the product.

Martin and Bill are both dads, too, and view their kids the same way they view cars at work. When Martin sees flaws in his children, he's continually surprised and upset. "Kids shouldn't be this way," he demands. Bill, on the other hand, sees similar weaknesses in his children but takes it in stride. He goes into one of his routines for helping his kids grow and develop.

Viewing your children as works in process instead of finished products can help you respond to them without harshness or frustration. Like Bill, you can view problems as opportunities. Misbehavior and relational struggles are indicators of where your child needs help to grow and mature.

Parents are often frustrated by the continual need for correction and the endless number of mistakes that kids make. If you can remember that your children are on the production line instead of in the showroom, your expectations will lead you to solutions instead of angry outbursts.

2. PARENTS MUST CHANGE FIRST

Some parents don't realize how serious the problem of parental anger really is. When confronted with their harshness, they say, "I wouldn't yell if my kids would just…" This kind of statement tries to place the cause of parental anger on the shoulders of children. There's no doubt that children do wrong things, respond poorly to correction, and have bad attitudes, but there's a better way to correct, instruct, and limit children. Remember, anger is good for identifying problems but not good for solving them. If you see yourself being easily provoked by your kids, maybe it's time to look at your own expectations before you begin trying to change your children.

There's nothing like a family to teach us how much growing we must do ourselves. Children reveal anger problems we never knew existed and show us habits of relating that have been ingrained for years. God can use our family to sanctify *us* and build the character in us that he desires. That look of fear or disappointment in our kids' eyes can cut to our hearts and provide the motivation for us to work harder on our own weaknesses. In one counseling session, Brian, a ten-year-old, said, "Sometimes I want to share problems with my dad, but I know he'll take the other side and start yelling at me. I wish we could be friends, but I hate it when he gets mad. We're really not very close." When his dad heard Brian's thoughts, he was struck with the truth that he needed to make some significant changes.

If you want to be at peace with yourself and with your kids, you're going to have to work at it. You can't just sit around and hope that you'll mellow out some day. Anger doesn't work that way. If you've developed patterns of angry behavior, now is the time to change. One single dad told us, "One morning, I got up, looked in the mirror, and didn't recognize the person I had become. I realized that I needed to make some changes in myself. Anger and bitterness were making me a hurtful person. As I began working on my own thoughts, feelings, and reactions, I was able to respond differently to life's struggles. I was then surprised to see my kids change in response to what they saw in me. Things started moving in a positive direction for my family."

Your transparency about your own weakness can be an encouragement to your kids. It's amazing how motivated to change a person becomes when he sees that others are in the same struggle—especially when those other people are his parents. You might say something like this to your child: "I'm open to any suggestions. I've never raised a Greg before. I'm doing the best I can, but if you have any ideas of ways I could discipline you more effectively, I'd like to hear them."

Don't be afraid to get help. Read books, talk to other parents, and take advantage of classes and seminars. Most importantly, study your children and learn how to parent from them. They have a surprising way of teaching us when we're coming on too strong or letting too many things go without correction.

Many parents have their anger meters set too tight. They react with intensity for even the smallest infraction of the rules. James 1:19-20 is helpful for us all to memorize: "Everyone should be quick to listen, slow to speak and slow to become angry, for man's anger does not bring about the righteous life that God desires." Character qualities like patience, persistence, and self-control help both children and parents to increase the tolerance level on their anger meter.

3. EXPECT RESISTANCE

In the movie *The Karate Kid,* Daniel comes to Mr. Miyagi to learn karate. Mr. Miyagi realizes that Daniel's goals are shortsighted, so he uses methods that confuse and surprise his young student. With very specific instructions, Mr. Miyagi teaches Daniel to wax the car, sand the deck, paint the fence, and paint the house. Daniel, not understanding the benefit of these exercises, begins to rebel, questioning the credibility of Mr. Miyagi and even suggesting that his teacher is using him as a slave to do his work. Only as Daniel matures is he able to see that the hard work Mr. Miyagi gave him produced skills that would help him face the biggest challenges of his life.

Just like Daniel in the movie, your children often won't understand why you instruct, correct, or limit them. They will, no doubt, question your wisdom and motivations. Although your children may resist your parenting, don't give up. There may be times when you'd rather escape than confront, rest than correct, or do the job yourself instead of instructing your children how to do it. You may have heard the story about the mom with three very active boys. One summer evening she was playing cops and robbers with them in the backyard after dinner. One of the boys "shot" his mother and yelled, "Bang! You're dead." She slumped to the ground, and when she didn't get up right away, a neighbor ran over to see if she had been hurt in the fall.

When the neighbor bent over, the overworked mother opened one eye and said, "Shhh. Don't give me away. It's the only chance I've had to rest all day."

Parents do need rest, but be careful that you don't neglect training your children just so you can do your own thing. Parenting requires sacrifice and work. Be courageous in challenging your children in spite of their resistance.

Hebrews 12:11 reminds us that discipline isn't easy to accept: "No discipline seems pleasant at the time, but painful." A child screams when he's about to get an immunization. He doesn't care whether it's going to prevent a disease or not; he just doesn't like pain. None of us wants pain in our lives. But discipline does involve pain. Whether we're doing physical therapy, trying to lose weight, or saving money, we must give up some things in order to gain something we want.

Be careful not to let resistance from your children get in the way of their training. Children don't usually have the foresight needed to work hard unless there's some kind of immediate reward. But then there are those occasional moments when your son brings in the trash cans without being asked or your daughter cleans up her room on her own. Those are the small indications that maturity is just around the corner. Encourage your children and determine to hang in there beyond the resistance. Your kids need your self-discipline and persistence as they grow to develop their own.

4. HARD WORK PRODUCES RESULTS

Some parents are afraid to say no to their children because they don't want to make them unhappy. All the other kids have a special kind of backpack, but your son has that same old plain blue one from last year. Do you buy him a new backpack? Maybe, but it's okay not to. Often children develop character by learning to live within boundaries.

The goal of parenting isn't to make children happy by giving them everything they want. It's okay for children to live within limits even though their friends don't. And it's all right for them not to have the latest gadgets or newest upgrades. What seem like terrible inconveniences to our children are often acts of love. You don't allow small children to play in the street or teenagers to stay out all night. You choose those limits to protect your kids.

Some children are restless. Like the prodigal son in Luke 15, their restlessness leads to defiance, rebellion, and wanting more than their family can offer. They steal, do drugs, or get involved in sex. Hebrews 12:11 says that discipline "produces a harvest of righteousness and peace." The child who acts out needs the peace that discipline provides. If a child doesn't learn the value of discipline at home, he'll have to learn it elsewhere in life in order to have the peace that overcomes restlessness.

A restless heart can be dangerous. Learn to detect the early warning signs of restlessness in your children. Stop the progression by exerting more discipline and focusing on character. How can you see it? Just look at the normal day-to-day interaction that we've addressed in this book. If your daughter isn't responding to correction, work on it. If your son can't accept a no answer, don't let it go. These children need character training. Children who accept discipline as something designed by their heavenly Father for their own good will cease to feel resentful and rebellious. But this doesn't come easily. As parents we need to be patient and consistent with our discipline.

There are two ways to learn something: experience and teaching. The prodigal son had to learn peace, contentment, and gratitude through experience. That's sad. Experience is often an unforgiving taskmaster. Too many adults have chronic diseases, injuries, or bad habits that are consequences of learning from experience. There's an easier way. When children learn lessons in the classroom of correction and instruction, they avoid much pain and suffering later in life.

The daily work of disciplining can build in children the character they'll need to be successful as they grow older. By focusing on the purpose and long-range benefits of discipline, you will be able to hang

---

Turn Frustration into Character

- When children learn to follow instructions they develop responsibility.
- When children learn to respond to correction they develop wisdom.
- When children learn to accept a no answer they develop contentment.
- When children learn how to have a good attitude they develop a positive outlook.
- When children learn restraint they develop self-control.
- When children learn honesty they develop integrity.
- And the list goes on and on. The time and energy you invest in parenting helps your children develop character.

---

in there, remain calm, and respond to problems with plans and solutions instead of reacting with anger.

THE CAMPING TRIP

My (Scott) family has enjoyed camping over the years. When our children were young, we frequently took tents and all our gear out to a campground to enjoy the outdoors for a couple of days. We cooked our meals over a fire and had a special time together away from the normal distractions of life.

Since my wife, Carrie, went camping with her family growing up, she had a number of suggestions for making our time successful. She had ideas that I never would have considered. For example, if you rub bar soap on the bottom of pans before using them over the fire, you will be able to clean the black soot off more easily. Hanging a container of food from a branch instead of leaving it on the ground protects the food from little wild animals that might come into the camp at night. And clothespins—never forget the clothespins! Not only can you hang up wet clothes; you can also use them for a number of handy troubleshooting solutions involving pinning things shut or holding things together. Carrie used many techniques and tips for making camping a fun and enjoyable time.

Of course, our kids loved camping too. They were eager to play in the woods, explore, build a fire, and just have fun. For the most part, they didn't even consider all the work and planning Mom did to make it a good experience.

Parenting is a lot like camping. As a mom or dad, you have the foresight to see what is coming down the road of life. You know that the way your son talks back will hinder his success. You know that your daughter's bad attitude at chore time is not only an irritation but, if not worked on, will make her an unhappy person. In the same way that Carrie's experience with camping helped her know how best to pack, your knowledge about life gives you insight into areas your kids need to work on in order for them to be successful.

Taking time to prepare your children for life doesn't mean you have to plan extra time to instruct them. Teach them in the course of daily activities. Use day-to-day interactions and relationships to help your children learn to be successful and develop character. Your kids may not appreciate it now, but as they get older they'll see the value of the things you've taught them.

THE GIFT OF A LIFETIME

Have you ever received a gift you didn't understand? You look it over, but it just doesn't make any sense. Many of the ways that God disciplines us as adults have surprises hidden within them. The trials and problems of life often teach us more than we ever imagined they could. Looking back we might even see them as gifts rather than burdens.

In each of these chapters, we have presented an aspect of parenting, and in each case, we have described discipline as a gift from you to your children. Although kids may not appreciate the gift or even recognize its value at the time, your understanding of your job will make your job easier. You give discipline, correction, instruction, and teaching to your children because you know it's what they need, not necessarily because they are going to enjoy it now or even understand why they're getting it.

As a parent, you have a responsibility to teach, guide, train, and lead your kids to the Lord and his principles of righteousness. Parents can pray that their children will change their hearts first so that behavior change will naturally follow, but change doesn't always happen that way. Sometimes a person must change behavior first so that God can change the heart. Just look at your own life. Maybe you've decided to stop yelling even though you still feel like blowing up. You change outwardly because you know it's the right thing to do, and you trust God to change your heart in time.

When beginning the work of parenting, many people think they know a lot and they'll quickly pick up what they don't know—but most of us usually get this parenting thing down about the time our grandchildren come along. It doesn't take long for us to realize that even when we're armed with the best strategies and plans, ultimately we can't control our children. We need the grace and mercy of a loving heavenly Father.

Take God up on the promise he gives in James 1:5: "If any of you lacks wisdom, he should ask God, who gives generously to all without finding fault, and it will be given to him." The time you spend in prayer will help you and your children grow in the Lord. Parenting is truly a spiritual experience, requiring faith, humility, and regular guidance from God. The routines you develop and your reliance on God's strength will bring positive changes to your whole family. When you're tempted to step into the boxing ring with your children and use harshness to "put this kid in his place," remember that you now can call upon new plans and routines. If your child tempts you to begin sparring, stay outside the ring and respond as a coach. View the verbal attacks as punches and commit to *not* punch back. Ask yourself, "What's the real problem here? How can I respond as a coach?" If you relate to your kids differently, they will have to adjust how they respond to you. Don't allow the struggles and immaturity your children experience to push you into your old ways of relating. Your kids need character, and you are the trainer.

Your anger has an important job. Use it to point out the areas of weakness in your children, then choose to respond with love, grace, and a helpful routine. Disciplining children is a walk of faith. Pray for wisdom, strength, and patience, realizing that your kids belong to

God and he is at work in their lives. He's using you as a tool to bring about growth and change in them. With care and planning, you can help your children develop the character that they need. In doing so, you'll give them a gift that will last forever.

PUTTING IT ALL TOGETHER

When You See...
Resistance in your children or discouragement in yourself, don't give up.

Move into a Routine...
Take time to remember why you're parenting. Recognize that children are on the production line, that parents must change first, that you can expect resistance, and that your hard work will produce results in the end.

Because...
Parenting isn't just for the moment. It prepares children for life.

QUESTIONS FOR FURTHER DISCUSSION

1. How can the production line/showroom illustration help parents reduce their angry responses?
2. Which one of the four suggestions in this chapter do you find to be the most motivating for you? Why?

DIGGING DEEPER

1. Read Hebrews 12:5-11. Give an example of when you've experienced discipline in your life from parents, other

adults, or God that was painful at the time although now
you see its benefits.

2. In Philippians 1:6 Paul encourages us with these words:
    "…being confident of this, that he who began a good
    work in you will carry it on to completion until the day
    of Christ Jesus." How does this verse apply to parents
    and to children and the way that we're all growing in
    family life?

BRINGING IT HOME

Have each family member identify one way he or she is trying to
improve family life. You might ask the question, "What are you working on that will add to our family and make it a better place to be?"
Be careful not to be critical. The question itself may raise an awareness of each person's need to grow.

About the Authors

Dr. Scott Turansky, D.Min., and his wife, Carrie, have five children and live in Lawrenceville, New Jersey. Dr. Turansky is a family coach and works with children and their parents each week. He directed a preschool for eight years and has been a pastor for over twenty years.

Joanne Miller, R.N., B.S.N., and her husband, Ed, teach their two boys at home. An author and public speaker, Mrs. Miller has been a pediatric nurse for seventeen years and is presently working at the Bristol-Myers Squibb Children's Hospital in New Brunswick, New Jersey.

ABOUT EFFECTIVE PARENTING

The Turanskys and the Millers founded the ministry of Effective Parenting in 1992. Effective Parenting is a nonprofit corporation committed to the communication of sound biblical parenting principles through teaching, counseling, and the publication of written, audio, and video materials.

Dr. Scott Turansky and Joanne Miller teach parenting seminars around the country. Their engaging presentation style includes drama, illustrations, and a dialogue teaching format. Many churches have taken advantage of their Parenting Seminar Outreach program to reach out to the community. Dr. Turansky and Mrs. Miller have written children's program material that can be used during the seminars so that churches can provide a ministry for the whole family. If you'd like to request a promo pack or learn more about the teaching ministry of Effective Parenting, please visit their Web site at www.effectiveparenting.org or call (800) 771-8334.

AND CHECK OUT THE NEW

Say Goodbye to Whining, Complaining, and Bad Attitudes... in You and Your Kids! Video Series

D r. Scott Turansky and Joanne Miller use drama, humor, stories, and illustrations to bring honor into the life of your family. Their video series includes thirteen, thirty-minute videos that give family members practical ways to put honor into practice.

Use this video series as part of the **Church Kit** that contains a leader's guide, a complete children's program for each session, and a book entitled *How to Run an Outreach to Your Community Using Parenting Classes.*

Or use this series as part of the **Family Kit** that contains a guide for family discussions and activities. Help your family grow from bad attitudes, meanness, and bickering into a family that honors one another.

Available in VHS or DVD

For more information, visit www.effectiveparenting.org or call Effective Parenting at (800) 771-8334.